Quality Estimation for Machine Translation

Synthesis Lectures on Human Language Technologies

Editor
Graeme Hirst, *University of Toronto*

Synthesis Lectures on Human Language Technologies is edited by Graeme Hirst of the University of Toronto. The series consists of 50- to 150-page monographs on topics relating to natural language processing, computational linguistics, information retrieval, and spoken language understanding. Emphasis is on important new techniques, on new applications, and on topics that combine two or more HLT subfields.

Quality Estimation for Machine Translation
Lucia Specia, Carolina Scarton, and Gustavo Henrique Paetzold
2018

Natural Language Processing for Social Media, Second Edition
Atefeh Farzindar and Diana Inkpen
2017

Automatic Text Simplification
Horacio Saggion
2017

Neural Network Methods for Natural Language Processing
Yoav Goldberg
2017

Syntax-based Statistical Machine Translation
Philip Williams, Rico Sennrich, Matt Post, and Philipp Koehn
2016

Domain-Sensitive Temporal Tagging
Jannik Strötgen and Michael Gertz
2016

Linked Lexical Knowledge Bases: Foundations and Applications
Iryna Gurevych, Judith Eckle-Kohler, and Michael Matuschek
2016

Quality Estimation for Machine Translation

Lucia Specia, Carolina Scarton, and Gustavo Henrique Paetzold

ISBN: 978-3-031-01040-8 paperback
ISBN: 978-3-031-02168-8 ebook
ISBN: 978-3-031-00179-6 hardcover

DOI 10.1007/978-3-031-02168-8

A Publication in the Springer series
SYNTHESIS LECTURES ON ADVANCES IN AUTOMOTIVE TECHNOLOGY

Lecture #39
Series Editor: Graeme Hirst, *University of Toronto*
Series ISSN
Print 1947-4040   Electronic 1947-4059

Quality Estimation for Machine Translation

Lucia Specia
University of Sheffield, UK

Carolina Scarton
University of Sheffield, UK

Gustavo Henrique Paetzold
Federal University of Technology – Paraná, Brazil

SYNTHESIS LECTURES ON HUMAN LANGUAGE TECHNOLOGIES #39

ABSTRACT

Many applications within natural language processing involve performing text-to-text transformations, i.e., given a text in natural language as input, systems are required to produce a version of this text (e.g., a translation), also in natural language, as output. Automatically evaluating the output of such systems is an important component in developing text-to-text applications. Two approaches have been proposed for this problem: (i) to compare the system outputs against one or more reference outputs using string matching-based evaluation metrics and (ii) to build models based on human feedback to predict the quality of system outputs without reference texts. Despite their popularity, reference-based evaluation metrics are faced with the challenge that multiple good (and bad) quality outputs can be produced by text-to-text approaches for the same input. This variation is very hard to capture, even with multiple reference texts. In addition, reference-based metrics cannot be used in production (e.g., online machine translation systems), when systems are expected to produce outputs for any unseen input. In this book, we focus on the second set of metrics, so-called Quality Estimation (QE) metrics, where the goal is to provide an estimate on how good or reliable the texts produced by an application are without access to gold-standard outputs. QE enables different types of evaluation that can target different types of users and applications. Machine learning techniques are used to build QE models with various types of quality labels and explicit features or learnt representations, which can then predict the quality of unseen system outputs. This book describes the topic of QE for text-to-text applications, covering quality labels, features, algorithms, evaluation, uses, and state-of-the-art approaches. It focuses on machine translation as application, since this represents most of the QE work done to date. It also briefly describes QE for several other applications, including text simplification, text summarization, grammatical error correction, and natural language generation.

KEYWORDS

quality estimation, quality prediction, evaluation, machine translation, natural language processing

Contents

Acknowledgments

The authors would like to thank the reviewers for their valuable feedback and Kim Harris for her comments and proofreading.

Lucia Specia, Carolina Scarton, and Gustavo Henrique Paetzold
August 2018

CHAPTER 1

Introduction

Quality Estimation (QE) for Natural Language Processing (NLP) applications is an area of emerging interest. The goal is to provide an estimate on how good or reliable the results returned by an application are without access to gold-standard outputs. This is therefore different from standard evaluation methods where the task is to compare system outputs with their gold-standard counterparts which are generally created by experts with knowledge of language. While NLP systems can be evaluated using gold-standard datasets and their average quality can be measured on those data points, it is known that the quality on individual outputs can vary considerably depending on a number of factors. QE is aimed at estimating the performance of a system on individual data points, rather than only overall system performance. The main motivation is to make applications more useful in real-world settings, where information on the quality of each output is needed and reference outputs are not available. QE approaches also have the advantage of allowing for a flexible modeling of the concept of quality, depending, among other things, on the user or intended use of the application's output.

QE approaches are normally framed as a supervised Machine Learning (ML) problem; therefore, the concept of quality can be implemented through specific labels used to train the models, as well as through specific features or representations extracted from the data. Generally speaking, this could be done for any application, for example part-of-speech tagging, parsing, or machine translation, but the need for QE becomes clearer in the context of applications that produce, as output, natural language. For such applications there is generally more than one possible "correct" output, and while it is easy to reason about what the output should look like, modeling this computationally is far from trivial. In this book, we target such applications and focus on describing methods and existing work that analyze the actual output of a system rather than the confidence of the system in producing this output. A related area that is also outside of the scope of this book is that of scoring or error detection in human texts, such as learner essays. While the general framework that is used to address QE of human texts can be similar to that for QE of automatic applications, texts written by humans involve issues in more varied dimensions of quality, which makes the two types of texts substantially different. We therefore focus on texts produced by automatic language output applications.

A question often asked about the motivation for QE is the following: If we can predict the quality of results returned by a particular system, why are we not able to modify the system *before* the system generates the output and thus avoid quality issues in the first place? As in many other research areas, estimating the existence of errors is a somewhat easier task than fixing them.

While it may be possible to identify that a text has issues, it may not be possible to pinpoint exactly which issues it has and—more important—to diagnose which parts of a system should be modified to prevent those issues from happening, especially when systems are complex, with at least a few components induced from data. In addition, given that an output has already been produced by the system, scoring it according to complex functions, such as using sophisticated linguistic information, is much more feasible than using such scoring functions during output generation process (referred to as *decoding* in many applications), where this information (i) may be too expensive to compute (i.e., running a syntactic parser over thousands of candidates) or (ii) not possible (i.e., the entire sentence is needed for the computation, which is only available at the end of the decoding process).

Among the various applications that generate natural language, arguably one of the most prominent in terms of number of users is Machine Translation (MT). There are various online systems that can be used for free (within a limited number of words) and are often embedded in other online software, in particular social media applications. It is estimated that Google Translate alone is used by 500 million people, translating more than 100 billion words everyday.[1] In the context of online MT systems, QE is clearly a useful tool to help users understand whether or not the translation provided can be trusted, especially when the speaker is not able to understand the source language. MT is clearly an area that can benefit from QE. In fact, most existing work in QE targets this application.

QE of MT has become increasingly popular over the last decade. Given a *source* language text and its machine translated version, which we often refer to as *target text*, the task of QE consists in providing a prediction on the quality of this machine translated text. QE systems have the potential to make MT more useful in a number of scenarios by, for example, improving post-editing efficiency by filtering out segments that require more effort to correct than to translate from scratch [Specia, 2011], selecting high-quality segments to be published as they are [Soricut and Echihabi, 2010], selecting a translation from either an MT system or a translation memory [He et al., 2010], selecting the best translation from multiple MT systems [Shah and Specia, 2014], and highlighting words or phrases that are not reliable and need attention and/or revision [Bach et al., 2011]. These examples of different applications of QE for MT cover the most popular levels at which predictions can be made: word, sentence or document. Figure 1.1 illustrates a possible interpretation of such levels, where for word-level QE a binary ("good"/"bad") label is predicted for each word, while for sentence or document-level QE a general quality score in [0, 1] is predicted (the higher the better). Variants of these levels of prediction include phrase and paragraph-level QE.

The majority of current work focuses on either word or sentence-level QE. In word-level QE a quality label is to be produced for each target word, e.g., a binary "good"/"bad" label or labels describing specific error types. A critical challenge is the acquisition of large training sets, since traditionally each word in such datasets needs to be labeled. Significant improvements

---

[1]https://blog.google/products/translate/ten-years-of-google-translate/

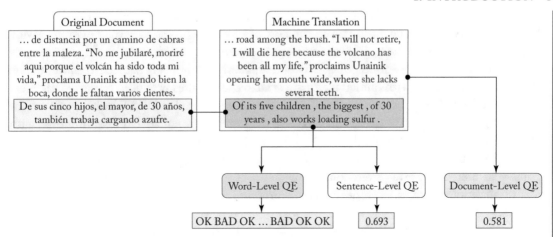

Figure 1.1: Different levels of translation quality prediction.

have been achieved since 2015 using neural network models and additional unlabeled training data, as we discuss in Chapter 2. Word-level QE has been covered in shared tasks organized by the Conference on Machine Translation (WMT) annually since 2013 [Bojar et al., 2013, 2014, 2017, 2016, 2015]. While most WMT13-14 QE shared task submissions were unable to beat a trivial baseline, in WMT15-17 most systems outperformed even stronger baselines, with the top systems doing so by a substantial margin.

Sentence-level QE is addressed using several supervised ML algorithms to induce models from examples of sentence translations described through a number of features (or learned representations) and annotated for quality using a variety of types of labels, e.g., 1–5 *Likert* scores. Sentence-level QE has been covered in shared tasks organized by the WMT annually since 2012 [Bojar et al., 2013, 2014, 2017, 2016, 2015, Callison-Burch et al., 2012]. Standard supervised ML algorithms can be used to build prediction models, with work on feature engineering having played a key role in this problem until very recently. In the last 2–3 years, with the popularisation of neural network approaches, the focus has shifted toward devising effective architectures that learn feature representations from the data, as we will discuss in Chapter 3. Since the second edition of the task, a significant proportion of the submissions has been outperforming a well known baseline by a large margin.

QE at other textual levels has received less attention. Document-level QE consists in predicting a single label for entire documents of variable lengths, be it an absolute score [Scarton, 2017, Scarton and Specia, 2014a] or a relative ranking of translations by one or more MT systems [Soricut and Echihabi, 2010, Soricut and Narsale, 2012]. The assumption is that the quality of a document is more than the simple aggregation of its sentence-level quality scores. While certain sentences are perfect in isolation, their combination in context may lead to an incoherent document. Conversely, while a sentence can be poor in isolation, when put in context, it may benefit from information in surrounding sentences, leading to a good quality document. Feature engineering is a challenge given the lack of processing tools to extract discourse-wide information, such as the topic and structure of the document and the relationship between its sentences. In addition, the notion of quality at document level is a very subjective concept. Few and very small datasets with human labels are available and scores produced by automatic metrics tend to be used as an approximation. This task was introduced at WMT in 2015 and ran for two years. Very few systems were submitted and the results were somewhat disappointing, with most systems performing similarly to a baseline that uses mostly sentence-level features. This is a hard variant of QE to address; nonetheless, its potential applications become increasingly popular as users move away from consuming sentence translations to consuming entire document translations, such as machine-translated product descriptions, product reviews, and news articles.

A variant of the word-level task that has been introduced more recently (WMT16-17) considers a phrase as a unit for quality prediction, as we will describe in Chapter 2. While a phrase could be defined as linguistically motivated, e.g., using a chunker [Blain et al., 2016], for the purposes of the shared tasks a phrase was defined as any sequence of one or more words that is handled by a statistical phrase-based MT system. This was done to avoid making the problem more complex by introducing the task of phrase segmentation. This definition of phrase is also appealing as it makes it feasible to use the predictions to guide decoding in statistical phrase-based translation systems. This task is not as well defined and harder to evaluate than word-level QE. Very few approaches have been proposed for it and it is likely to become obsolete given that the vast majority of MT systems now follow neural models, where the unit of translation is a sentence that is generated word by word, rather than phrase by phrase.

Having different levels of prediction is important for different applications. While most applications would probably benefit from sentence-level predictions, e.g., for the decision on whether or not to post-edit a sentence, some applications require more fine-grained, word or phrase-level information on quality. For example, one may want to highlight words that need fixing or inform readers of portions of a sentence that are not reliable. Document-level QE is needed particularly for *gisting* purposes, where post-editing is not an option.

This book provides an introduction to the field of QE focusing on MT as a language output application and covering all the aforementioned levels of prediction. It is structured such that one chapter is dedicated to each prediction level: Chapter 2 describes **subsentence-level MT QE**, covering word and phrase-level prediction, Chapter 3 focuses on **sentence-level MT QE**, and Chapter 4 introduces **document-level MT QE**. All chapters follow a similar structure, containing an introduction to the prediction level, its applications, labels, features, and models used, and finally evaluation methods and state-of-the-art results. Chapter 5 presents an **overview of QE for other NLP applications**, more specifically, Text Simplification (TS), Automatic Text Summarization (ATS), Grammatical Error Correction (GEC), Automatic Speech Recognition (ASR), and Natural Language Generation (NLG).

CHAPTER 2

Quality Estimation for MT at Subsentence Level

2.1 INTRODUCTION

MT systems can make various types of errors during translation. Systems can fail to disambiguate words correctly and subsequently fail to capture the meaning of the source text, omit important words from the source, make grammatical errors such as incorrect verb and noun inflection, or fail to find a suitable translation to a given word, to name a few. Take, for example, the Portuguese-English translation case in Table 2.1, produced by Google Translate.[1]

Table 2.1: Example of sentence translation from Portuguese to English with one word error

SRC (PT)	As configurações deste computador são bárbaras!
MT (EN)	The specs of this computer are barbaric!
PE (EN)	The specs of this computer are terrific!

In this example, the MT system failed to capture the fact that "*bárbaras*", which can mean "*barbaric*" in some contexts, is used as a slang in this Portuguese sentence. In this context, "*bárbaras*" means "*terrific*" or "*excellent*". Notice, however, that if it were not for this mistake, Google Translate would have produced a perfect translation: The sentence does not contain any grammatical errors, and every word aside from "*barbaric*" perfectly reproduces the meaning of the source sentence. For this example, an effective sentence-level QE method would produce a numerical score that informs the user that the translation is of good quality overall, but contains errors nonetheless. However, it would not be able to tell which parts of the sentence contain such errors, nor the kind of error they are. It was in an effort to address these limitations that the tasks of word and phrase-level QE were conceived.

In word-level QE, the input is a translation along with the source sentence and the output is a sequence of labels, one for each word of the translation. Each label will indicate the quality of the word in question. A translated word that has been incorrectly translated would ideally receive a label that represents such an error.

[1]https://translate.google.com

Suppose that there is a sentence-level QE system that produces a quality score between 0 and 1, where 1 represents a perfect translation, and a word-level QE system that labels correctly translated word as "G" (for "good"), and incorrectly translated words as "B" (for "bad"), regardless of the type of error made. These systems would produce an output similar to what is illustrated in Figure 2.1 for the translation example in Table 2.1.

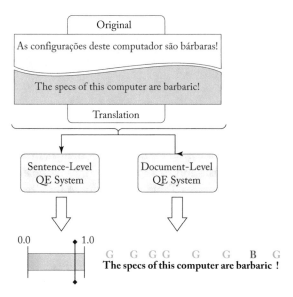

Figure 2.1: Comparison between sentence and word-level QE systems.

Even though the word-level quality labels used here are simple binary labels, they already allow for a more insightful analysis of the translation quality than the sentence-level score. A phrase-level QE system would operate in the same way, the only difference being that it would provide a label for each phrase identified in the sentence, rather than each word. The main goal behind phrase-level QE is to label errors as they are produced: An error cannot always be isolated from other words in its context, especially for MT systems that translate phrases as a unit, and therefore considering an entire phrasal construct, such as a multi-word expression or compound noun, as a unit of prediction is a reasonable assumption.

In QE work, phrases are often obtained from the MT systems themselves. Phrase-based MT models, for example, natively employ phrase segmentation. Most neural translation models, however, tend to treat the sentence being translated as a single sequence of tokens, which makes it more challenging to infer phrasal constructs. In this case, methods to automatically identify multi-word expressions and other compound constructs could be used for phrase segmentation.

The foundational concepts of word and phrase-level QE were laid back in 1996 by Schürmann [1996], who addressed confidence estimation for pattern recognition. Soon after, Fetter et al. [1996] introduced the use of confidence measures in the task of rescoring word graphs in speech recognition models in order to improve their reliability. Many similar contributions appeared after that, such as those of Bergen and Ward [1997] and Chase [1997], which focused on analyzing and improving the performance of speech recognition with confidence estimates. Gandrabur and Foster [2003], Ueffing and Ney [2004], and Blatz et al. [2004] introduced QE in translation tasks, which was referred to as "confidence estimation". Ueffing and Ney [2007] established the first framework for word-level QE. Their contribution fostered numerous others both within the context of MT, such as in Bach et al. [2011], de Gispert et al. [2013], Xiong et al. [2010], as well as in other contexts, such as parsing [Goldwasser et al., 2011, Reichart and Rappoport, 2009].

Another major milestone in the history of word-level QE was the introduction of the first shared task on this prediction level, WMT13 [Bojar et al., 2013]. In this shared task, teams were asked to submit binary and 4-class predictions by word-level QE systems for the English-Spanish language pair. Since then, word-level QE shared tasks continue to be hosted yearly at WMT [Bojar et al., 2014, 2017, 2016, 2015], and in 2016 that a phrase-level QE shared task was introduced. The latter focused on predicting the quality of phrase-based machine translations for English-German.

In what follows, we describe the various aspects of word and phrase-level QE, such as their applications (Section 2.2), quality labels and features used for training (Sections 2.3 and 2.4), architectures (Section 2.5), evaluation methods (Section 2.6), and state-of-the-art approaches (Section 2.7).

2.2   APPLICATIONS

The earliest application of word-level QE is in the context of ASR, where the task is more frequently referred to as *word confidence estimation*. Simply put, the task of ASR consists in transforming an audio signal containing spoken language into its equivalent textual representation. As pointed out by Jiang [2005], quality estimates, otherwise known as *confidence estimates* in the context of ASR, can aid the performance of speech recognizers in various ways. The purpose of a word confidence estimator is to quantify how confident a speech recognizer is that each predicted word in the textual output is actually being said during a certain portion of the spoken audio input. One of the most popular applications of confidence estimates can be found in word graph decoding. A word graph, such as depicted in Figure 2.2, is a data structure that describes the array of hypothetical sentences that can represent the speech excerpt that is being recognized. The task of speech recognizers—called *decoding*—consists in finding a suitable hypothesis in the word graph. In Figure 2.2, a hypothesis that is very likely to be suitable is the sentence "*The shoe is on the other foot*", since this is a more common sentence in the English language than any of the other candidates.

To search for a "good" hypothesis, speech recognizers can assign a confidence estimate to each of the words in the graph, then employ a decoding algorithm to find the best sentence based on a given optimization metric. By investigating different ways of calculating such confidence

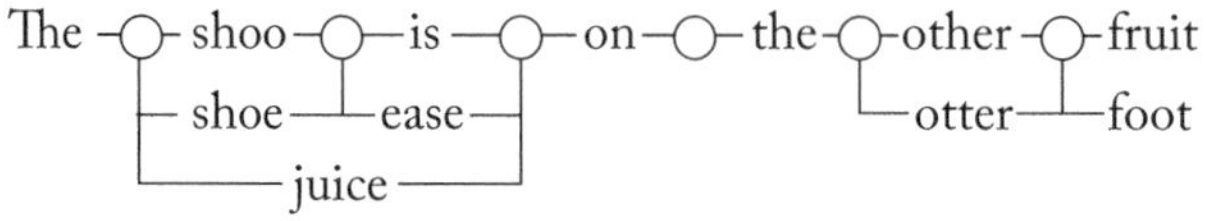

```
The ─○─ shoo ─○─ is ─○─ on ─○─ the ─○─ other ─○─ fruit
        shoe ─── ease                 otter    foot
              ─── juice ───
```

Figure 2.2: Example of word graph generated by a speech recognition model.

estimates, researchers have been able to effectively push the performance of ASR models. The work of Fetter et al. [1996] and Wessel et al. [2000] are some examples of that. Confidence estimates have also been successfully employed in many other processes inherent to ASR, such as stack search [Neti et al., 1997], out-of-vocabulary word filtering [Jitsuhiro et al., 1998], and utterance verification [Lleida and Rose, 2000]. There have also been efforts in directly predicting the quality of audio utterances as a whole [Negri et al., 2014] in order to facilitate the process of deciding which automatically produced text transcriptions are of acceptable quality.

Analogously to what has been done in the context of ASR, word-level QE has also been employed in order to improve the performance of MT systems. Much like speech recognizers, many MT models, such as phrase-based models, include a step of decoding in order to find a suitable translation hypothesis for a given source sentence based on a translation word lattice. The word lattice has the same structure as the word graphs previously described for ASR. Word- and phrase-level quality estimates have been used to better guide the process of decoding in phrase-based [Kumar et al., 2009, Tromble et al., 2008], syntax-based [Venugopal et al., 2007, Zhang and Gildea, 2008], and neural MT (NMT) [Chatterjee et al., 2017, Rikters and Fishel, 2017].

Another approach used in MT is that of reranking: The model produces a list of candidate translation hypotheses from the graph, then reranks them using another method in order to determine which of them should ultimately be chosen. Word-level quality estimates have been successfully used in reranking to improve the performance of MT systems [Luong et al., 2014b, Zhang et al., 2006].

Finally, word- and phrase-level QE systems have great potential use in industry as well. As discussed in Section 3.2, one of the main applications of sentence-level QE systems is helping human translators to decide what course to take when manually correcting a translation: Is it good enough to be kept as is? If not, is it good enough for post-editing? However, as discussed in Section 2.1, sentence-level systems offer a rather vague notion of quality, not allowing for the human translator to immediately know which parts of the translation are "good" or "bad". Word and phrase-level approaches can hence further improve post-editing workflows by offering more informative labels including, potentially, not only the words that are incorrect but also the types of errors that need correction.

2.3   LABELS

Word- and phrase-level QE for MT are often framed as a classification task, using discrete labels for training and prediction. Sometimes, however, the classification task is framed in a probabilistic fashion, such as in the case of word confidence estimation for ASR. The earliest examples of word- and phrase-level quality labels were confidence estimates for ASR [Fetter et al., 1996]. Fetter et al. [1996] use Equation (2.1) to define a confidence estimate to rescore the words in a word graph:

$$P_w\left(C|s_w\right) = \left(1 + \frac{P_w\left(s_w|E\right)}{P_w\left(s_w|C\right)} \frac{P_w\left(E\right)}{P_w\left(C\right)}\right)^{-1}. \tag{2.1}$$

In Equation (2.1), C represents the class of correctly predicted words, and E the class of errors made by the recognizers. P_w represents the confidence that a word w was correctly predicted (and hence is in class C) conditioned on s_w, which is the original score of word w in the word graph. $P_w\left(s_w|C\right)$ and $P_w\left(s_w|E\right)$ are the inverse probabilities of the original score s_w with respect to classes C and E, and $P_w\left(C\right)$ and $P_w\left(E\right)$ are their prior probabilities. Since this equation follows the probabilistic principles of the Bayes rule, the quality estimate P_w is hence a continuous floating-point value between 0 and 1.

As discussed by Jiang [2005], continuous confidence estimates can be calculated in a number of ways, but in most cases they are produced in unsupervised fashion, i.e., without the help of any manually annotated data. The estimates are usually incorporated within the probabilistic framework that allows speech recognizers to perform crucial steps in the recognition process, such as word graph decoding and utterance verification. Ultimately, the continuous confidence estimates are used for binary classification: The ASR system uses them to decide which words will be part of the transcription, and which will not.

All WMT shared tasks on word-level QE employ discrete labels. In these tasks, QE is not framed as a tool for another end task, like for ASR, but is instead the end task itself. The datasets used for the first word-level QE shared task, held at WMT13, featured the English-Spanish language pair. Each instance was composed by a source sentence in English, its machine translation in Spanish, and two different sets of discrete labels.

- **Binary:** Each word receives either a "keep" (K) or "change" (C) label, where a "change" label represents words that should be corrected in the translation. This corresponds to a "good"/"bad" distinction.

- **Multi-class:** Each word receives either a "keep" (K), "delete" (D) or "substitute" (S) label, where "delete" and "substitute" represent words that should be edited in the translation in order for it to be correct.

In order to obtain these labels, the task organizers resorted to a technique that relies on post-editing. First, they obtained post-edited versions for each translation in the training and test sets. These post-edited versions are corrected versions of the machine translations edited by professionals. They then employed a tool that automatically calculates the Translation Error Rate (TER) between the machine translation and the post-edited version (i.e., Human-targeted Translation Edit Rate (HTER)). The TER score is calculated based on the smallest number of word deletions and substitutions necessary in order to transform the machine translation into the post-edited version. This process yields not only a numerical score, which is the TER itself that represents the minimum edit distance between the two versions, but also a label for each word in the machine translation, indicating which words should be changed.

A subset of TER labels (deletions and substitutions) were used in their raw form for the shared task's multi-class and grouped into two labels to create "good"/"bad" labels for their binary setting. Figure 2.3 shows an example of a translation from the shared task's training set with both label sets. This example also highlights an important limitation of TER-inferred word-level QE labels. The post-edited version featured in Figure 2.3 is considerably longer than the translation. This is due to the fact that the human post-editor felt the need to not only remove and substitute some words in the machine translation, but also add the segment "*comparten este punto de vista,*" which means "*share this point of view,*" in order for it to appropriately capture the meaning of the source. Since word-level QE only assigns labels to words that actually occur in the machine translation, additions such as these cannot be represented.[2]

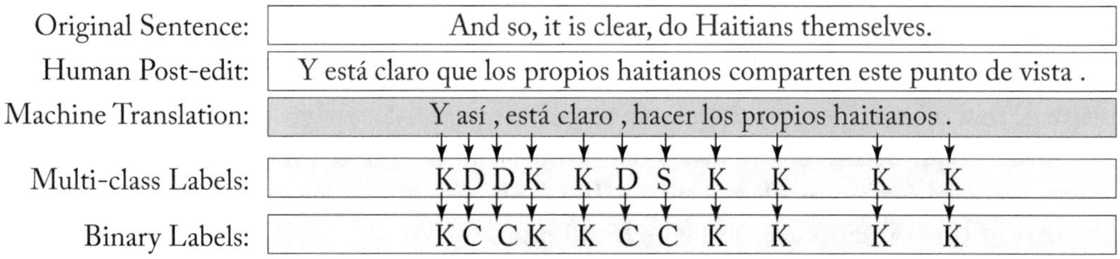

Original Sentence:	And so, it is clear, do Haitians themselves.
Human Post-edit:	Y está claro que los propios haitianos comparten este punto de vista .
Machine Translation:	Y así , está claro , hacer los propios haitianos .
Multi-class Labels:	K D D K K D S K K K K
Binary Labels:	K C C K K C C K K K K

Figure 2.3: Multi-class and binary word-level QE labels for an instance of the WMT13 training set.

WMT14 held a word-level QE shared task that used a different set of quality labels. Instead of collecting human post-edits and automatically inferring word-level labels through TER, they employed professional human annotators to identify and categorize the different types of errors made by the MT systems. The error categorization used is a subset of the Multidimensional Quality Metrics (MQM) [Lommel et al., 2014], which is illustrated in Figure 2.4. They also addressed more language pairs: English-German, German-English, English-Spanish, and Spanish-English.

Based on the MQM scheme, they annotated each translation in their datasets with three label sets.

---

[2]The word-level QE shared task of WMT18, which was yet to happen at the time of writing this book, addresses this limitation by providing annotations that allow QE systems to predict error labels for missing words.

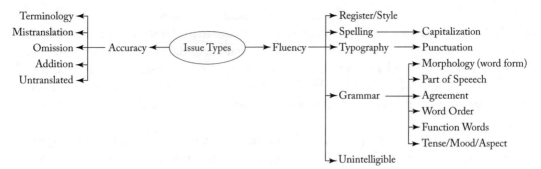

Figure 2.4: MQM error typology.

- **Multi-class:** Each mistranslated word is labeled with one of the fine-grained error categories in the MQM scheme (capitalization, punctuation, terminology, mistranslation, omission, etc).

- **Level 1:** Mistranslated words are labeled with the coarse-grained error categories in the MQM scheme (accuracy and fluency).

- **Binary:** Translated words are labeled as either "good" or "bad".

Level 1 labels were inferred from the multi-class labels by simply generalizing them in their coarse-grained error categories, and binary labels were generalized from the level 1 labels by simply grouping every label that represents an error in the "bad" category. Figure 2.5 illustrates an instance from the WMT14 shared task Spanish-English training set. It should be noted that each word in the phrase "*of 30 years*" received an individual "register/style" label. They are shown as a single label here for presentation purposes.

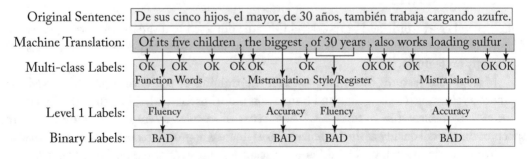

Figure 2.5: QE labels for an instance of the WMT14 training set.

Using a fine-grained label set can potentially make the output produced by the QE system much more informative for human translators. However, using fine-grained label sets also increases the complexity of the problem, since the estimator needs to capture more subtle nuances between a broad array of error types. This generally requires more labeled data, which was not the case in the WMT14 shared task: The same number of data points were provided for all prediction levels. The results reported for the task highlight the impact of this complexity. For example, the F1 scores (described in detail in Section 2.6) obtained by the submitted systems for the binary, level 1 and multi-class labels in the Spanish-English language pair averaged 0.26, 0.20, and 0.06, respectively.

Because the annotation process used to collect the WMT14 datasets was complex and the scores obtained for the finer-grained label sets were rather low, the subsequent WMT15, WMT16, and WMT17 word-level QE shared tasks featured only binary "good" and "bad" label sets collected through the previously described post-editing-based approach used in WMT13.

The first phrase-level QE shared task was held at WMT16 and it was framed as an extension of the word-level QE task. The training and test sets used for the phrase and word-level tasks were the same, the only difference being that word-level datasets contained one label for each word and phrase-level datasets one label for each phrase in the translation. Since the MT systems used to produce the sentences for the datasets were phrase-based statistical systems, inferring phrasal constructs could be done easily. The phrase segmentation as used by the MT systems decoders was taken and used to segment the sentences.

The phrase labels were inferred using a very simple method: If any of the words that compose a phrase has a "bad" label in the word-level dataset, the phrase is assigned a "bad" label. This approach works under the premise that any type of word-level error spans across the entirety of the phrasal construct of which it is a part. This is a fair premise if one intends to replace or fix or replace entire phrases, for example, when using quality estimates to guide decoders in MT systems. Other, less pessimistic approaches have also been suggested as alternatives, for example, labeling as "bad" only phrases in which at least 50% of the words are labeled as "bad".

2.4   FEATURES

In the general case, word- and phrase-level QE are addressed in a supervised setting, in which ML models are built using data produced by human annotators. Supervised QE models rely very heavily on features.

Most of the features commonly used in the training of sentence-level QE models are continuous values such as language and translation model probabilities, length and token count ratios, etc., as discussed in Section 3.4. These types of features attempt to capture important aspects of the overall quality of the sentence such as fluency, appropriateness, and grammaticality.

Word- and phrase-level QE differ significantly from sentence-level QE in that respect. The features used for these QE variants focus much more on localized pieces of information that pertain specifically to the neighborhood of the word or phrase. These features are often also more specific, and for that they need to be lexicalized. Models are thus trained not only with continuous but also with discrete features.

Discrete features are features whose value can be only one in a closed set of possible values. A discrete word-level feature could be, for example, the bigram composed of the labeled word and its subsequent word in the translated sentence, while an analogous continuous feature could be the raw frequency of this bigram in a language model. Notice that for this particular discrete feature the set of possible values would be the bigram vocabulary of the target translation language.

Based on the source sentence and its machine translation counterpart, a number of continuous and discrete features have been proposed to capture the quality of words and phrases in context. Some of them focus exclusively on either the source or target side of the translation, and some exploit the interactions between the two. As discussed in Section 3.4, we categorize features that exploit the source sentence and translation as "complexity" and "fluency" features respectively, those that exploit the relationship between them as "adequacy" features and those that reflect the confidence of the MT system as "confidence" features. We present the discrete and continuous features that have been most frequently used in the creation of supervised word- and phrase-level QE models.

2.4.1   WORD-LEVEL FEATURES

Discrete features are the most popular for word-level QE. They can be found in almost every approach submitted to the WMT shared tasks on word-level QE [Bojar et al., 2013, 2014, 2017, 2016, 2015]. In order to illustrate features, we will use the Portuguese-English translation in Figure 2.6. Along with the translation itself, we also include part-of-speech (POS) tags for the source and translation, dependency relations for the translation, and word alignments between the sentences.

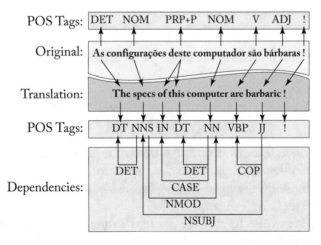

Figure 2.6: Portuguese-English translation with POS tags and dependencies.

Fluency Features

Suppose we are calculating features for the word *computer* in the translation of Figure 2.6. We will refer to it henceforth as our "target word". Some of the most widely used discrete fluency (or target-side) features for it are:

- target word itself: *computer*;

- POS tag of the target word: *NN*;

- bigrams including the target word: *this computer, computer are*;

- POS bigrams including the target word: *DT NN, NN VBP*;

- bigrams composed of the target word and the POS tags of its surrounding words: *DT computer, computer VBP*;

- trigrams including the target word: *of this computer, this computer are, computer are barbaric*;

- POS trigrams including the target word: *IN DT NN, DT NN VBP, NN VBP JJ*; and

- trigrams composed of the target word and the POS tags of its surrounding words: *IN DT computer, DT computer VBP, computer VBP JJ*.

These features describe the target and its surrounding context and can potentially help the QE system associate certain lexical patterns with a given quality label. A language model can be used to calculate the probability of these n-grams as well, and hence produce continuous features. If the target word is part of an n-gram with a high probability in a language model, then it is less likely that it constitutes a grammatical error, for example.

Other popular continuous features that can be calculated with language models are:

- length of the longest n-gram to the left/right of the target present word in the language model, and

- length of the longest POS n-gram to the left/right of the target word present in the tagged language model.

The intuition behind these features is similar to that of n-gram language model probabilities: The higher the length of known n-grams in the translation, the less likely it is that the MT system made a mistake. A POS-tagged language model is a language model trained over the POS tags of the sentences in a given corpus.

Language models can also be used for discrete feature extraction. Raybaud et al. [2011] conceived a feature called the "language model backoff behavior", which looks at the bigram and trigram composed by the target word and the words preceding it in order to categorize the target word with respect to the presence or absence of n-grams in the language model. This feature is described by Equation (2.2), in which $B(w_i)$ is the backoff behavior of the i-th target word w_i in a sentence.

$$B(w_i) = \begin{cases} 7, & \text{if } w_{i-2}w_{i-1}w_i \text{ is in the language model} \\ 6, & \text{if } w_{i-2}w_{i-1} \text{ and } w_{i-1}w_i \text{ are in the language model} \\ 5, & \text{if only } w_{i-1}w_i \text{ is in the language model} \\ 4, & \text{if } w_{i-2}w_{i-1} \text{ and } w_i \text{ are in the language model} \\ 3, & \text{if } w_{i-1} \text{ and } w_i \text{ are in the language model} \\ 2, & \text{if only } w_i \text{ is in the language model} \\ 1, & \text{if } w_i \text{ is out of the vocabulary.} \end{cases} \quad (2.2)$$

The concept behind the backoff behavior features is simple: The larger the value obtained, the less likely it is that the target word constitutes an error in the translated sentence, since its surrounding context is more strongly represented in the language model. A variant is to look at the n-grams of the POS tags rather than the words themselves.

Some binary word class indicators are also popular discrete features. They capture whether or not the target word should be treated in a special manner by the QE system. Proper nouns, for example, are correctly translated (or copied from the source) more often than not, hence the estimator can be more optimistic about them. Popular binary features are as follows.

- Is it a stop-word?

- Is it a punctuation symbol?

- Is it a proper noun?

- Is it a numeral?

For our example target word *computer*, the answer to these questions would be "no". Dependency parses can also yield very useful fluency features. The word-level QE model of Martins et al. [2016], which achieved the highest scores in the WMT16 shared task, is trained with various features that combine the information from the dependency relations and POS tags of the translation in question. In order to illustrate these features with respect to the target word *computer*, we must refer to its syntactic head word and grand-word. In Figure 2.6, the head word of *computer* is *specs*, since it is from *specs* that comes the incident dependency relation *NMOD*, and the head grand-word of *computer* is *barbaric*, since it is from *barbaric* that comes the dependency relation *NSUBJ* incident to *specs*. We also define the target's dependency siblings as the words to which the target is either directly or indirectly connected through dependency relations. The main dependency features used by Martins et al. [2016] are:

- dependency relation between the target word and the head word, and its concatenation with the target word itself: *NMOD, NMOD+computer*;

- concatenation of the target word, the head word and their respective POS tags: *computer/NN+specs/NNS*;

- concatenation between the target word, its closest sibling to either its left or right in the sentence, and their respective POS tags: *computer/NN+this/DT, computer/NN+barbaric/JJ*; and

- concatenation between the target word, the head word, the head grand-word, and their respective POS tags: *computer/NN+specs/NNS+barbaric/JJ*.

Another important fluency feature that relies on dependency parses is the "null link" feature [Xiong et al., 2010]. It is a binary feature that receives value 1 if there is at least one dependency relation between the target and another word in the sentence. In all other cases it receives a value of 0. Hence, if the dependency parser cannot associate a given target word with any other word of the translation, it is very likely that it constitutes an error. As illustrated in Figure 2.6, our example target word *computer* is part of various dependency relations, and hence this feature would receive value 1.

Pseudo-reference translations can also be used to calculate fluency features. For word-level QE, pseudo-reference features are binary and receive value 1 if a given target word is present in the pseudo-reference in question, and 0 otherwise. The intuition is that if the target word appears in a translation produced by a different MT system, then it is likely that it does not constitute an error. Multiple pseudo-references can also be used to make this information about consensus: The larger the number of pseudo-references the target word appears in, the less likely an error it is. These features tend to disregard any information on position of the target word in the pseudo-references with respect to its position in the machine translated sentence.

Finally, there are also numerous semantic features that have been used in QE systems [Martins et al., 2017a, Shah et al., 2015b, Tezcan et al., 2015]. By using lexical databases such as WordNet [Miller, 1995] and BabelNet [Navigli and Ponzetto, 2012], it is possible to calculate features such as the number of senses, synonyms, hypernyms, or hyponyms for the target word. If no such databases are available, distributional semantic models can be exploited instead, such as the skip-gram and bag-of-words models in word2vec [Mikolov et al., 2013a]. From these models, word embeddings for the target word can be extracted and used as features directly. As discussed in Section 3.4, modern QE approaches are moving away from feature engineering and toward these word representations, since they manage to capture interesting properties of words, can be seamlessly incorporated in neural architectures, and can be obtained from raw, unlabeled text. Section 2.7 demonstrates the most effective word- and phrase-level QE approaches to date use these representations exclusively as input features [Kim et al., 2017b].

Complexity Features

Using similar resources and techniques, a number of features that exploit cues about the source sentence being translated can also be calculated. Since these features generally attempt to indicate how challenging it was for the MT system to translate the source sentence, they are often referred to as complexity features. Many of these features rely on word alignments between the source sentence and its machine translation, which can be obtained as a by-product in statistical MT (SMT) systems. In the previous example in Figure 2.6, the target word *computer* is aligned with *computador*, which is its direct translation in Portuguese. Using this link between them, various features can be extracted, including:

- source word aligned to the target word: *computador;*

- POS tag of the source word aligned to the target word: *NOM;*

- bigrams including the source word: *deste computador, computador são;*

- bigram POS tags including the source word: *PRP+P NOM, NOM V;*

- bigrams composed of the source word aligned to the target word and the POS tags of its surrounding words: *PRP+P computador, computador V;*

- trigrams including the source word: *configurações deste computador, deste computador são, computador são bárbaras;*

- trigram POS tags including the source word: *NOM PRP+P NOM, PRP+P NOM V, NOM V ADJ;* and

- trigrams composed of the word aligned to the target word and the POS tags of its surrounding words: *NOM PRP+P computador, PRP+P computador V, computador V ADJ.*

Notice that because all the information these features use can be produced after the translation is produced (mainly alignments, n-grams, and POS tags), systems that exploit them can still be considered black-box QE approaches. QE systems use these features in an attempt to identify patterns within the source sentence that are likely to lead to errors in the MT system. If the QE system observes that the trigram *"deste computador são"* is commonly associated with "bad" quality labels in the training data, for example, it could become more pessimistic about the quality of the words aligned to it in the translation.

Adequacy Features
Adequacy features aim to combine information from both source and target sentences. Their primary aim is to capture how adequate the translation is with respect to the source provided. It does so by capturing the relationship between the target word being analyzed and its context within the source sentence being translated. Adequacy features for word-level QE that could be calculated for the target word *computer* in Figure 2.6 include:

- bigrams composed of the target word and the words in the source sentence surrounding the word aligned to it: *deste computer, computer são;*

- bigram POS tags of these words: *PRP+P NN, NN V;*

- bigrams composed of the target word and the POS tags of words in the source sentence surrounding the aligned word: *PRP+P computer, computer V;*

- trigrams composed of the target word and the words in the source sentence surrounding the word aligned to it: *configurações deste computer, deste computer são, computer são bárbaras;*

- trigram POS tags of these words: *NOM PRP+P NN, PRP+P NN V, NN V ADJ;* and

- trigrams composed of the target word and the POS tags of words in the source sentence surrounding the aligned word: *NOM PRP+P computer, PRP+P computer V, computer V ADJ.*

There are also binary adequacy features that can capture important quality clues by comparing the target word and its aligned word in the source sentence, for example [Tezcan et al., 2015].

- Are both the target word and its aligned word identical? No: *Computer* is not identical to *computador.*

- Are both the target word and its aligned word content words? Yes: *Computer* is a noun (NN) and so is *computador* (NOM).

- Are both the target word and its aligned word function words? No: Both of them are content words.

Confidence Features

Interesting continuous confidence features can be calculated, using the translation probability tables produced by SMT models. These tables list the prior probability that a given word will be translated into another. For example, the probability that *computador* will be translated into *computer* is much higher than the probability of it being translated into *chair*, or *love*. Common features extracted from these tables are:

- translation probability between the word aligned to the target and the target itself;

- number of translations for the target word with a probability over α; and

- number of translations for the word aligned to the target with a probability over α.

It is very intuitive to see how these features could help a QE system. If the translation probability between the aligned word and the target is too small, for example, then there is a good chance that the MT system made a mistake. Also, if the number of translations with probability above a certain threshold α available for the aligned word is very high, then there is a higher chance that the MT system made a mistake, since there are many ways in which it could have translated the word. Different values for α will lead to variants of these features.

2.4.2   PHRASE-LEVEL FEATURES

Since word- and phrase-level QE are very similar in principle, many of the word-level features described in the previous section can be used in the creation of phrase-level QE systems. Word alignments can be used to infer alignments between phrases in the translation and in the source sentence, subsequently allowing fluency, complexity, adequacy, and confidence features to be adapted.

Logacheva et al. [2016a] adapt various word-level features for phrase-level QE. To illustrate them, consider as example the translation illustrated in Figure 2.7, which was taken from the WMT16 datasets for German-English translation.

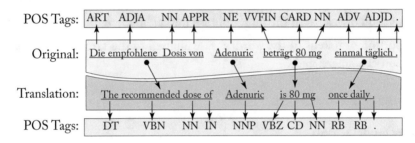

Figure 2.7: German-English translation with POS tags.

Given the target phrase "*is 80 mg*", aligned to "*beträgt 80 mg*" in Figure 2.7, the following context features can be extracted:

- words preceding and succeeding the target phrase: *Adenuric, once;*

- POS tags of these words: *NNP, RB;*

- words preceding and succeeding the aligned phrase: *Adenuric, einmal;*

- POS tags of these words: *NE, NN;*

- whether there are named entities in the target phrase: *No;* and

- whether there are named entities in the source phrase: *No.*

Using a vocabulary and a language model, adapted versions of important word-level features can also be extracted in a content-aware fashion, such as:

- existence of a word in the source phrase that is out of the vocabulary;

- length of the longest n-gram present in the language model to the left of the first word in the target phrase (*is*);

- length of the longest n-gram present in the language model to the right of the last word in the target phrase (*mg*);

- language model backoff behavior with respect to the first word of the target phrase and its two preceding words (“*of Adenuric is*”); and

- language model backoff behavior with respect to the last word of the target phrase and its two succeeding words (“*mg once daily*”).

Phrase-level QE also has many similarities with sentence-level QE. Like sentences, phrases are composed of more than one word and can be of arbitrary size. Many continuous sentence-level features have been employed in phrase-level QE, for example:

- **Punctuation features:**

    - proportion of tokens in the target phrase that are punctuation characters;
    - proportion of tokens in the word/phrase aligned to the target phrase that are punctuation characters; and
    - difference in number of punctuation characters in the target phrase and the aligned word/phrase.

- **Language model features:**

    - number of tokens in the target phrase;
    - number of tokens in the word/phrase aligned to the target phrase;
    - average length of tokens in the target phrase;
    - average length of tokens in the word/phrase aligned to the target phrase; and
    - ratio between the number of tokens in the target phrase and its aligned word/phrase.

- **Alignment features:**

    - number of words in the target phrase that are not aligned to any word in the source sentence;
    - number of words in the target phrase aligned to more than one word in the source sentence; and
    - average number of alignments between the words in the target phrase and the words in the source sentence.

- **Part-of-speech features:**

    - percentage of content words in the target phrase;
    - percentage of content words in the aligned word/phrase;
    - percentage of nouns/verbs/adjectives/adverbs/numerals/pronouns in the target phrase;

  - percentage of nouns/verbs/adjectives/adverbs/numerals/pronouns in the word/phrase aligned to the target phrase; and

  - ratio of nouns/verbs/adjectives/adverbs/numerals/pronouns between the target phrase and its aligned word/phrase.

Multi-level prediction features can also be exploited to model the relationship between phrase-, word- and sentence-level QE. Given a sentence-level QE model that predicts HTER scores and a word-level QE model that produces binary "good"/"bad" labels, the following features can be extracted:

  • quality label produced by the sentence-level QE model;

  • number of words in the target sentence predicted as "good"/"bad" by the word-level model; and

  • number of words in the target phrase predicted as "good"/"bad" by the word-level model.

These features could help the model learn to be more pessimistic toward the phrases that compose a sentence with a low quality score, for example, or to be more optimistic about a given phrase if all words it contains have been predicted as "good".

2.5   ARCHITECTURES

Supervised word- and phrase-level QE models are trained on a set of machine translations annotated with labels derived from human annotation. These labels are often discrete, although probabilistic methods can be used to infer models that output a probability score on the correctness of a word or phrase. For feature extraction, approaches can resort to external tools and resources such as POS taggers, parsers, language models, translation probability models, and pseudo references. For model learning, since both word- and phrase-level QE tasks consist in estimating a sequence of quality labels rather than a single label for a sentence, different architectures can be used. We describe three types of architectures: non-sequential, sequential, and automatic post-editing-based approaches.

2.5.1   NON-SEQUENTIAL APPROACHES

Non-sequential approaches are arguably the simplest way to address word- or phrase-level QE. These approaches predict the labels of each word/phrase in the analyzed sentence independently from the predictions of other words/phrases. In other words, they do not exploit the fact that the words in a sentence constitute a sequence, and that there may be interdependencies in the way labels are assigned.

In Figure 2.8, which illustrates the application of a typical non-sequential QE approach, the target word is *barbaric* in the machine translated sentence *"The specs of this computer are barbaric!"* After relevant features are extracted for this word, a trained non-sequential ML model estimates the quality label of the target word in question.

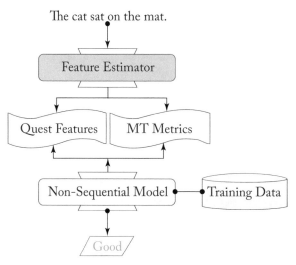

Figure 2.8: Architecture of a non-sequential QE approach.

The only information available as input to a non-sequential model are the features that describe the target word itself. The model does not take advantage of the quality predictions it has made for other target words in the past, since it assumes that they are not related to the respective target word. However, this does not mean that the non-sequential model is oblivious to the context in which the target word is inserted: As discussed in Section 2.4, the features that represent the target word can capture many aspects of its context, such as the words surrounding it, its POS tag, its dependency relations with other words, etc.

Many standard ML classifiers can be used to train non-sequential models. These include random forest classifiers, which learn an ensemble of decision trees over the training data [Esplà-Gomis et al., 2016, Singh et al., 2013], multi-layer perceptrons, i.e., a neural model composed of various stacked layers of feed-forward nodes [Esplà-Gomis et al., 2015, Tezcan et al., 2016], support vector machines (SVM) [Rubino et al., 2013], and many other classifiers. While these have shown competitive performance in the past, in recent evaluation campaigns non-sequential models have been outperformed by sequential alternatives. For example, in contrast with the first place obtained by Esplà-Gomis et al. [2015] in WMT15, the improved version of the models in Esplà-Gomis et al. [2016] placed seventh in the word-level QE shared task in WMT16.

By disregarding the fact that the words in a sentence are part of a sequence, non-sequential approaches ignore important information regarding the interdependencies between them. As demonstrated by the datasets provided for the WMT word- and phrase-level shared tasks, machine translations often feature various sequences of incorrectly translated words. A verb disambiguation error, for example, could lead an MT system to mistranslate the object of such a verb. If a QE model is able to find a disambiguation error at a given point of a translation, it could in theory exploit this information in order to more accurately capture subsequent inter-dependent errors. Non-sequential models are also incapable of performing any form of "global" optimization of the sequence of quality labels with respect to the sentence as a whole, which is something many sequential models attempt to do.

One of the biggest drawbacks of non-sequential models is the fact that they do not offer effective ways to address long-distance relationships between the words in a sentence. Although not all sequential models are capable of doing so, some sequential models are, such as long short-term memories (LSTMs). Consider, for example, the Portuguese-English translation featured in Figure 2.9, which contains human-produced "G" labels for properly translated words, and "B" labels for translation errors. The English translation would be perfect if not for the wrong choice of pronoun made by the MT system.

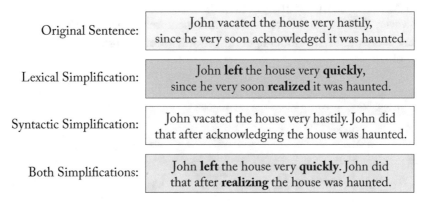

Figure 2.9: Portuguese-English translation with an error.

If this annotated translation were to be part of a training set for word-level QE, non-sequential models would have a difficult time learning how to assimilate the fact that the feminine pronoun *she* should not be associated with the word *man*. As discussed in Section 2.4, most of the features commonly used to create approaches for word- and phrase-level QE focus only the information pertaining to the target word's close vicinity, such as its two preceding and succeeding words. Since *man* is six tokens apart from *her* in the translation, and non-sequential models are not directly aware of the sequence to which *her* belongs, it becomes very difficult for these models to capture this particular clue. One could try to address this problem by simply using longer n-grams as features, for example, but this would most likely be ineffective since the non-sequential model used would have difficulty handling the inherent sparsity of long n-grams. Also, since sentences can be many times larger than the one illustrated in Figure 2.9, it would be challenging to even decide how long the n-grams should be. An alternative would be to calculate a feature that captures the relationship between the gender of pronouns and the subject to which they pertain in the sentence. But this is a complex task, since pronoun gender is only one of the many types of long-distance relationships that can be found within sentences, which means that an extensive feature engineering process would have to be undertaken in order for a non-sequential model to address all of them.

2.5.2   SEQUENTIAL APPROACHES

As the name suggests, a sequential QE approach takes word- or phrase-level QE as a sequence labeling problem. In other words, it takes advantage of the fact that the words being labeled are part of a sequence, namely the sentence. Sequential approaches seek to determine which sequence of quality labels best represents the quality of multiple words in a sentence.

Figure 2.10 illustrates the overall way in which a simple sequential QE approach operates. Its structure is quite similar to that of a non-sequential approach, the only difference being that it uses a sequential ML model that can predict the label of a target word by taking into account the words preceding it, as well as the predictions that it has made for them. It is important to mention, however, that this architecture does not accurately represent the exact way in which each and every sequential ML model operates, it only offers insight into the overall way these models are applied.

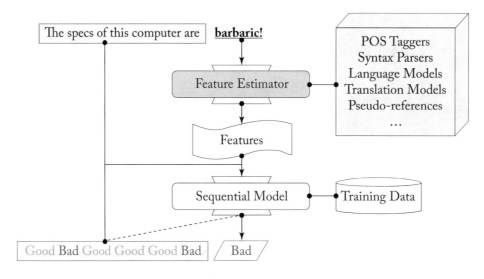

Figure 2.10: Architecture of a sequential QE approach.

Sequential QE approaches constitute the majority of systems submitted to the word and phrase-level QE shared tasks held at WMT conferences. One of the sequential models most frequently used to create these approaches are conditional random fields (CRFs) [Lafferty et al., 2001]. In general terms, a CRF can be described as a discriminative undirected graph model where each random variable $y_i \in \{y_1, y_2, ..., y_{n-1}, y_n\}$ is represented by a node conditioned on an input observation X. In word- and phrase-level QE, X represents the input sentence, and each y_i represents a quality label to be predicted. CRFs are similar to generative Hidden Markov

Models (HMMs) [Stratonovich, 1960] in the sense that they are also bounded by the Markov assumption: The value of any variable in the graph is conditioned on the value of its neighbors. In other words, in order to determine the value of a certain node in the graph, one needs only to know the value of the nodes directly adjacent to it.

Because they are graph models, CRFs are inherently flexible and can take different shapes depending on the task being addressed. In parsing tasks, for example, CRFs can take the shape of the syntactic tree nodes themselves. In tasks characterized by linear sequences, such as word- and phrase-level QE, linear-chain CRFs can be used, as illustrated in Figure 2.11.

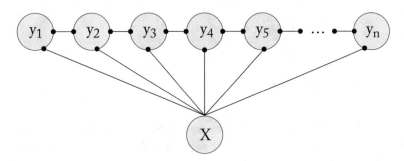

Figure 2.11: A linear-chain CRF model.

Word-level CRF models used to be very popular and performed well in early work and shared tasks, placing first and second in WMT13 [Luong et al., 2013]. However, they were outperformed by other approaches from WMT14 [Luong et al., 2014a, Shang et al., 2015]. The same applies for phrase-level CRFs [Logacheva et al., 2016a]. Interestingly, no CRF systems were submitted to either the WMT17 word- or phrase-level shared tasks, other than the baseline systems provided by the task organizers, which placed between fourth and eighth across all settings. CRFs have recently been replaced by another kind of sequence model: Recurrent Neural Networks (RNNs).

Neural networks are models composed of interconnected nodes commonly organized in layers. A complete neural model is composed of three types of layers: input, output, and hidden. Figure 2.12 illustrates a simple neural model. It has one input layer with two nodes, three hidden layers with four nodes, and one output layer with a single node.

The behavior and applicability of a neural model can be influenced by a number of design decisions, such as the number of layers and nodes used and the arrangement of connections between nodes, but arguably the most important of all aspects is the type of nodes used. recurrent neural networks (RNNs) are variants of neural models characterized by recurrent nodes that are appropriate for structured prediction tasks such as sequence labeling.

Suppose the information pertaining to a given target word X_i in a translation is being passed onto a recurrent neural node in a hidden layer. The node will apply a transformation to this information and produce a hidden representation H_i. A non-recurrent node would simply

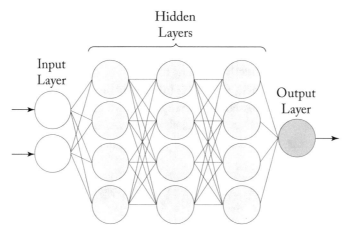

Figure 2.12: A simple neural model.

pass H_i as input to the connected nodes in the next layer, but a recurrent node would also pass H_i as input to itself when calculating the representation H_{i+1} for the next target word X_{i+1}. Figure 2.13 illustrates this.

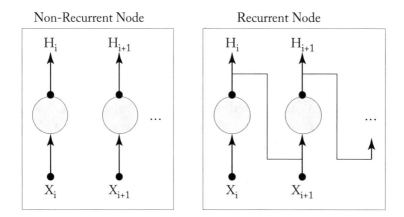

Figure 2.13: Functioning of a recurrent neural node.

Variants of these recurrent nodes have been proposed. Gated recurrent units (GRUs) [Cho et al., 2014] and LSTM nodes [Hochreiter and Schmidhuber, 1997] are the two most popular choices for word- and phrase-level QE approaches. The RNN model by Camargo de Souza et al. [2014] was the first to use this architecture for QE. They use LSTMs and achieve first place in the WMT14 word-level QE shared task for binary labels. In the most recent task editions, RNNs were used by all winning submissions for word- and phrase-level QE [Kim and Lee, 2016, Kim et al., 2017b, Martins et al., 2016], as we discuss in Section 2.7.

2.5.3   APE-BASED APPROACHES

A substantially different approach for word- and phrase-level QE is the use of Automatic Post-Editing (APE) for these tasks. As previously discussed, PE has been extensively used to label words and phrases for model training by:

1. manually producing post-edited versions of the translations through human annotation;

2. calculating the TER between the translation and its post-edited version; and

3. transforming the keep/delete/substitute labels onto a set of quality labels.

For phrases, once word-level QE labels are produced, phrase segments in the translations are identified and word-level labels are transformed into phrase-level labels by assigning "bad" to each phrase with at least one word with a "bad" label, and "good" to the rest.

APE-based QE approaches exploit this process to tackle word and phrase-level QE. Figure 2.14 illustrates how APE-based QE approaches operate. Instead of attempting to learn how to label words and phrases directly, an APE-based approach attempts to learn how to post-edit machine translations. Once that is done, TER can be computed and labels can be extracted in the same way. Its main component is the automatic post-editor, which is not trained with quality labels, but rather post-edited versions of machine translations. Datasets such as those provided for recent WMT shared tasks contain not only source sentences, their machine translations and quality labels inferred through TER, but also the post-edited versions of machine translations used to calculate TER labels. In addition, to build effective APE modules, other datasets with post-edited translations can and have also been used for training, including synthetically generated data via back-translation.

Martins et al. [2017a] present a hybrid QE approach that combines different types of linear, neural, and APE-based models trained with a wide array of features. Their best-performing system substantially outperforms the other participating systems in the WMT16 word-level task [Bojar et al., 2016]. Hokamp [2017] introduces an APE-based QE approach that combines various APE systems trained with recurrent neural models and a much lighter set of features than the one used by Martins et al. [2017a]. Their approach achieves second and third place in the WMT16 and WMT17 word-level QE shared tasks, respectively [Bojar et al., 2017].

APE-based approaches can be effective if the post-editing model is reliable. The main limitation of these approaches is the fact that they cannot be employed (on their own) for non-binary prediction tasks, where more detailed error types are to be predicted.

2.6   EVALUATION

The context in which a word or phrase-level QE approach is applied is an important factor in its evaluation. If QE is the end task and there is an evaluation dataset available, common classification evaluation metrics can be used. On the other hand, if the QE approach is to be

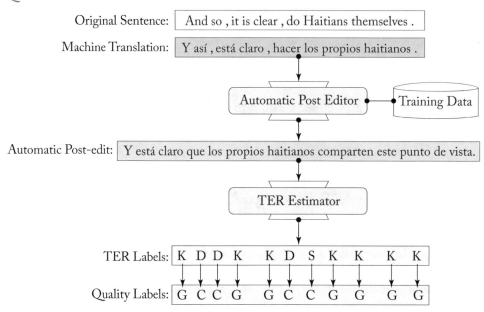

Figure 2.14: Architecture of an APE-based QE approach.

used as part of a solution for another end task, extrinsic evaluation methods for the task at hand would be needed to assess how the QE approach affects the results of the end task.

The shared tasks held at WMT events have served as main benchmarks for dedicated word- and phrase-level QE approaches. Labels used in the WMT tasks are all discrete: Either binary "good"/"bad" labels, multi-class "keep"/"delete"/"substitute", or MQM labels. Classification tasks are commonly evaluated using metrics like precision, recall, and F-measure. Precision measures the proportion of correct predictions made for a certain class with respect to the total number of predictions made for that class, while recall measures the proportion of correct predictions made for a certain class with respect to the total number of instances with that class in the evaluation dataset. The F-measure is calculated as the harmonic mean between precision and recall. For the "bad" class in a binary "good"/"bad" setup, for example, these metrics can be calculated via (2.3), (2.4), and (2.5):

$$\text{Precision (``bad")} = \frac{\text{correct ``bad" predictions}}{\text{correct ``bad" predictions} + \text{incorrect ``bad" predictions}} \qquad (2.3)$$

$$\text{Recall (``bad")} = \frac{\text{correct ``bad" predictions}}{\text{correct ``bad" predictions} + \text{incorrect ``good" predictions}} \qquad (2.4)$$

$$\text{F-measure ("bad")} = \frac{2 \cdot \text{precision ("bad")} \cdot \text{recall ("bad")}}{\text{precision ("bad")} + \text{recall ("bad")}}. \tag{2.5}$$

Up until WMT15, word-level systems were ranked based on the F-measure, more specifically, the F-measure for the "bad" class. Given that the vast majority of words in the datasets have a "good" label, predicting a "bad" label is the biggest challenge for systems. Hence, the choice for F-bad as the primary metric. In order to avoid favoring extremely pessimistic approaches, including dummy systems that classify all words as "bad", a new metric was introduced by Logacheva et al. [2016c]: the F-mult score. F-mult is the product between the F-measure for "good" and the F-measure for "bad" classes, as illustrated in Equation (2.6). This metric favors neither pessimistic nor optimistic approaches. It is better than the standard F-measure for both classes as it will ensure a score of 0 or very low for any system that over predicts either "good" or "bad" labels:

$$\text{F-mult} = \text{F-measure ("good")} * \text{F-measure ("bad")}. \tag{2.6}$$

F-mult cannot be directly applied, however, in settings where words can receive more than two types of labels, i.e., in multi-class classification setups. Bojar et al. [2014] address this problem using the average F-measure, which consists of the weighted multiplication of the F-measure for all possible labels. In Equation (2.7), which describes the average F-measure for a set of N quality labels, α_i is calculated as the proportion with which label L_i appears in the task's datasets. This weighting scheme accounts for the fact that the distribution of labels in multi-class QE setups is often heavily skewed toward a small group of labels:

$$\text{Average F-measure} = \sum_{i=1}^{N} \alpha_i \cdot \text{F-measure} (L_i). \tag{2.7}$$

For phrase-level QE, evaluation can be done in the same way: either treating each phrase as a unit and counting correct and incorrect labels for that unit [Bojar et al., 2017], or assigning the label predicted for each phrase to all words in the phrase and performing word-level evaluation [Bojar et al., 2016].

It is only possible to assess if (and to what extent) a QE system performs well in another end task if its presence improves (by how much) the performance of this end task, using metrics specific to that task. Besacier et al. [2015] evaluate the effectiveness of their word-level QE approach in guiding the decoding process of an MT system by looking at the BLEU scores produced. If an MT system achieves a higher BiLingual Evaluation Understudy (BLEU) score by using their QE approach as opposed to not using it, the QE model offers an improvement to the translation model.

There are, however, other ways of assessing the impact of QE approaches incorporated as part of another end task. In order to decide which "good"/"bad" quality label to assign to a certain word in a sentence, for example, a QE approach can apply a threshold t to a continuous probabilistic quality score. If the score is greater than t, then the word will receive an "good" label; otherwise, it will receive a "bad" label. If the goal is to compare the performance of two QE approaches, one could simply choose a threshold t and then calculate the resulting F-mult, for example, for each one of them. The problem is that different choices of t could lead to different verdicts on which QE approach is better. To address this problem, Receiver Operating Characteristic (ROC) curves can be used. As discussed in Section 3.6, an ROC curve consists of a plot between the rate of true and false positives with respect to a large set of increasing continuous t values between 0 and 1. This true positive rate (TPR) and the false positive rate (FPR) can be calculated as:

$$\text{TPR} = \frac{\text{Number of correctly predicted positives}}{\text{Number of positives in the test set}} \tag{2.8}$$

$$\text{FPR} = \frac{\text{Number of incorrectly predicted positives}}{\text{Number of negatives in the test set}}. \tag{2.9}$$

Figure 2.15 illustrates an example of an ROC curve. Each point in the curve represents a TPR/FPR coordinate with respect to a certain threshold value. Good-quality estimates should create a curve that "walks" as closely as possible to the upper-left corner of the graph, since that corner represents the association between a high TPR and a low FPR. Looking at Figure 2.15, for example, "QE method 2" is clearly the most effective approach.

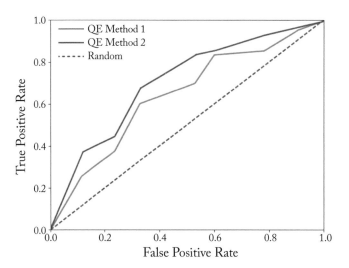

Figure 2.15: Example of an ROC curve.

Another example of an evaluation plot that could be used is the Detection Error Tradeoff (DET) curve [Martin et al., 1997], which allows better insight into the types of errors made by the QE approach. DET curves plot the previously introduced false positive rate (FPR) against the false negative rate (FNR), which is calculated as:

$$FNR = \frac{\text{Number of incorrectly predicted negatives}}{\text{Number of positives in the test set}}. \qquad (2.10)$$

Notice that these methods can be used to evaluate not only QE approaches incorporated as part of MT systems, but also word confidence estimation approaches incorporated into ASR systems.

2.7   STATE-OF-THE-ART RESULTS

WMT shared tasks have been instrumental in comparing both word- and phrase-level QE approaches. In what follows we describe the three most successful approaches for word-level QE: The predictor-estimator for word-, phrase-, and sentence-level QE [Kim et al., 2017b], and the hybrid models for word- and sentence-level QE [Martins et al., 2017a], and the APE-based approach by Hokamp [2017]. These models have achieved the highest performance in WMT15-17 by using sophisticated sequential architectures. Before that, we show how these compare to other approaches in the most recent WMT campaigns.

In the latest edition of the WMT shared task, participants were encouraged to evaluate their approaches using not only the current edition's datasets, but also datasets from the 2016 edition. The training set in 2017 is a superset of that in 2016, produced by the same MT system, for the same text domain and annotated in the same way. This way, it was possible to quantify progress over time and check whether the winning approaches perform well on the task in general, or if they just happened to perform well on a specific dataset. Results showed that most WMT17 systems perform better than the ones submitted in 2016. The winning submission at WMT16 was outperformed by four WMT17 systems, and the majority of WMT16 systems performed closely to the WMT17 baseline system (which we note is the same model in 2016 and 2017, but uses more training data in 2017). We refer the reader to the report from WMT17 for more detailed results [Bojar et al., 2017].

2.7.1   THE PREDICTOR-ESTIMATOR APPROACH

Kim et al. [2017b] introduced an effective approach that achieved first place in every variant of the word-, phrase-, and sentence-level QE shared tasks of WMT17. It is a sequential approach that uses RNN models in a very sophisticated way. The models are called predictor-estimators, because they are composed of two major components: a predictor, which predicts words based on the context in which they appear; and an estimator, which produces quality estimates for words and phrases. The predictor uses an encoder-decoder RNN model, and the estimator uses a typical unidirectional RNN model. By attempting to predict words, the predictor produces various important context representations that are used as input by the estimator, which in turn is able to produce quality estimates.

Before we delve into how the predictor and the estimator details, we define some key components that will be referred to throughout the text that follows.

- $\mathbf{x} = (x_1, x_2, ..., x_n)$: A sequence of n one-hot vectors that describe the source sentence being translated.

- $\mathbf{y} = (y_1, y_2, ..., y_m)$: A sequence of m one-hot vectors that describe the machine translation sentence.

- y_j: The jth target word in the machine translation $\mathbf{y}$.

- $\mathbf{y}_\leftarrow = (y_1, y_2, ..., y_{j-1})$: The context that precedes the target word y_j in the translation $\mathbf{y}$.

- $\mathbf{y}_\rightarrow = (y_{j+1}, y_{j+2}, ..., y_m)$: The context that succeeds the target word y_j in the translation $\mathbf{y}$.

The predictor will receive as input y_j, $\mathbf{x}$, $\mathbf{y}_\leftarrow$, and $\mathbf{y}_\rightarrow$, and attempt to predict the probability that y_j is expected to be found in the jth position in $\mathbf{y}$. The predictor does not need QE data to be trained: It can simply be trained over any parallel corpus of the language pair being addressed. Kim et al. [2017b] train the predictor over large corpora such as Europarl [Koehn, 2005]. The predictor's architecture is illustrated in Figure 2.16. Its main components are as follows.

- Ex_j: The embedding vector of the jth word in the source sentence $\mathbf{x}$, produced by an embedding layer.

- Ey_j: The embedding vector of the jth word in the machine translation $\mathbf{y}$, produced by an embedding layer.

- h_j: The hidden representation of the jth word in the source sentence $\mathbf{x}$, produced by an RNN layer.

- $s_j^\rightarrow$: The hidden representation of the jth word in the machine translation $\mathbf{y}$, produced by a forward RNN layer.

- $s_j^\leftarrow$: The hidden representation of the jth word in the machine translation $\mathbf{y}$, produced by a backward RNN layer.

- c_j: The source sentence context vector for the jth word in the machine translation $\mathbf{y}$, produced by the attention layer placed over the encoder.

- C_o, V_o, and S_o: Matrices that regularize different pieces of information to the same dimensionality so that they can be easily combined through summation.

- $\tilde{t}_j$: An intermediate representation that encompasses various pieces of contextual information regarding the jth word in the machine translation $\mathbf{y}$.

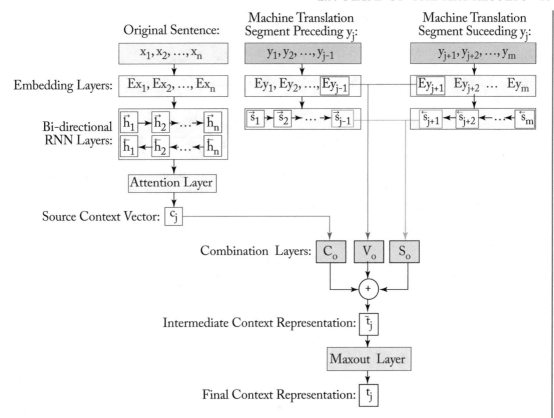

Figure 2.16: **Architecture of the** Kim et al. [2017b] **predictor.**

- t_j: The final representation of the contextual information of the jth word in the machine translation **y**.

The predictor first encodes the information from the source sentence onto c_j using a bi-directional RNN model with the attention layer. It then combines c_j with two other pieces of information: the embeddings of the words that immediately precede (Ey_{j-1}) and succeed (Ey_{j+1}) the target word y_j, and their hidden representations $s_{j-1}^{\rightarrow}$ and $s_{j+1}^{\leftarrow}$. These are produced, respectively, by a forward RNN layer that processes the translation segment that precedes y_j ($\mathbf{y}_{\leftarrow}$), and a backward RNN layer that processes the segment that succeeds it ($\mathbf{y}_{\rightarrow}$). This combination is performed by matrices C_o, V_o, and S_o through the summation illustrated in Equation (2.11):

$$\tilde{t}_j = C_o c_j + V_o \left[Ey_{j-1}; Ey_{j+1} \right] + S_o \left[s_{j-1}^{\rightarrow}; s_{j+1}^{\leftarrow} \right]. \tag{2.11}$$

These three combination layers produce outputs with the same dimensionality, which allows for them to be summed. This process results in $\tilde{t}_j$, which is then passed onto a maxout layer [Goodfellow et al., 2013] which calculates t_j using Equation (2.12):

$$t_j = \left[\max\left\{\tilde{t}_{j,2k-1}, \tilde{t}_{j,2k}\right\}\right]_{1 \leq k \leq l}^{\top}.$$ (2.12)

With t_j at hand, the predictor can then calculate the probability $p(y_j \mid \mathbf{x}, \mathbf{y}_{\leftarrow}, \mathbf{y}_{\rightarrow})$ using Equation (2.13):

$$p(y_j \mid \mathbf{x}, \mathbf{y}_{\leftarrow}, \mathbf{y}_{\rightarrow}) = \frac{\exp\left(y_j^{\top} W_{o1} \odot W_{o2} t_j\right)}{\sum_{v \in V} \exp\left(v^{\top} W_{o1} \odot W_{o2} t_j\right)}.$$ (2.13)

In Equation (2.13), W_{o1} and W_{o2} are two additional matrices of parameters learned by the model that combine y_j and t_j, and v is a one-hot vector representation of a given word in vocabulary V. Notice that y_j is also a one-hot vector representation.

The output probability distribution $p(y_j \mid \mathbf{x}, \mathbf{y}_{\leftarrow}, \mathbf{y}_{\rightarrow})$ is used for the training of the predictor, but it is not passed onto the estimator as input. Instead, using some of the byproducts from the predictor, QE feature vectors (QEFVs) are calculated. Two types of QEFVs are defined: Pre-prediction (Pre-QEFV) and post-prediction (Post-QEFV), which are calculated as shown in Equations (2.14) and (2.15).

$$\text{Pre-QEFV}_j = y_j^{\top} W_{o1} W_{o2} t_j$$ (2.14)

$$\text{Post-QEFV}_j = \left[s_j^{\rightarrow}; s_j^{\leftarrow}\right].$$ (2.15)

Pre-QEFV vectors are part of the numerator of Equation (2.13) and represent the most fundamental piece of information in calculating $p(y_j \mid \mathbf{x}, \mathbf{y}_{\leftarrow}, \mathbf{y}_{\rightarrow})$. Post-QEFV vectors, on the other hand, are the concatenation between the jth hidden states produced by the forward and backward RNN models that encode $\mathbf{y}_{\leftarrow}$ and $\mathbf{y}_{\rightarrow}$ respectively. Note that Post-QEFVs encompass information that is not used in the calculation of $p(y_j \mid \mathbf{x}, \mathbf{y}_{\leftarrow}, \mathbf{y}_{\rightarrow})$, which is why they are called "post-prediction" feature vectors.

Kim et al. [2017b] calculate and concatenate Pre- and Post-QEFV vectors for each target word in a given machine translation and then send them as a sequence to the estimator, which then assigns quality labels to them. The estimator has a much simpler architecture than the predictor: It is a simple bi-directional RNN model that takes as input QEFVs and produces word-, phrase-, and sentence-level quality labels as output. Figure 2.17 illustrates the architecture of the estimator.

Kim et al. [2017b] train a model on the WMT17 QE shared task datasets using a multi-task learning setup. These datasets provide labels for word, phrase, and sentence on the same set of translations. In order to connect the estimator to the predictor, a technique called stacked propagation is used, which allows for the information learned by the estimator to be propagated back to the predictor. The Kim et al. [2017b] submission to the WMT17 shared tasks was not a single predictor-estimator, but rather an ensemble of 15 model variants. These variants

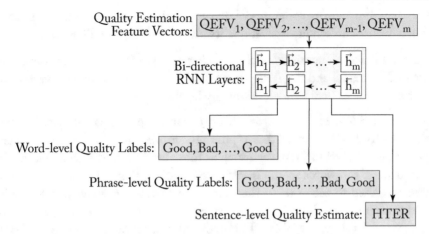

Figure 2.17: Architecture of the Kim et al. [2017b] estimator.

use different embedding, vocabulary, and hidden layer sizes. These variants are combined by averaging their output.

Using this approach, Kim et al. [2017b] achieve the best results in the official competition for both word, phrase and sentence-level QE 2017.

One of the main features of this work is the way a typical RNN model trained over QE data (the estimator) can be complemented with a powerful underlying model that learns from much more abundant data (the predictor). Collecting QE labels is an expensive process; hence, this approach makes the task more cost-effective. Another positive aspect of this work is that it does not resort to any form of feature engineering. While the predictor takes as input automatically learned embedding representations, the estimator takes as input vectors automatically produced by the predictor.

The main drawback of a predictor-estimator approach is its inherent complexity. The model is composed of several parts that can be configured and structured in numerous ways, and the training process requires significant experience with neural sequential models and hyperparameter optimization.

2.7.2   UNBABEL'S HYBRID APPROACH

Martins et al. [2017a] introduce a hybrid word and sentence-level QE approach that outperformed former state-of-the-art approaches submitted to WMT15 and WMT16 QE shared tasks by up to 13.36% in Pearson's *r* for sentence-level QE. This hybrid approach combines three components:

- an RNN model that interleaves recurrent layers with feed-forward layers for word-level QE;

- an APE-based encoder-decoder model that automatically post-edits a machine translation and infers word- and sentence-level quality estimates based on TER; and

- a word-level linear sequential model that takes as input the word-level output of the sequential RNN model and the APE-based model, combines them with various other features, then produces final word-level quality labels.

The architecture of the Martins et al. [2017a] hybrid approach is illustrated in Figure 2.18. The word-level RNN model is referred as a "pure QE" model, since it is trained exclusively over manually created word-level QE datasets, such as those used in WMT shared tasks. It takes as input four sequences: the words in the machine translation, their POS tags, the words in the source sentence aligned to each one of them, and their POS tags as well. It learns individual embeddings for each one of these input sequences, passes them onto a series of RNN layers, then produces word-level quality labels. The predicted proportion of "bad" word-level labels is used as sentence-level quality estimate.

The APE-based model is described in detail in Section 2.7, as it was also used by Hokamp [2017]. Two post-editors named SRC→PE and an MT→PE are trained, which take as input the source sentence and the machine translation, respectively, and produce as output a post-edited version of the machine translation. Martins et al. [2017a] train these models over artificially produced machine translations combined with WMT shared task data up-sampled 20 times. The quality labels produced by these two models are combined by taking their weighted sum. The weights are fine-tuned with respect to a given evaluation metric, for example, those used in WMT15 and WMT16 shared tasks. The resulting model produces a TER score between the machine translation and its post-edited version, as well as a sequence of word-level quality labels extracted from the TER calculation process.

The word-level linear sequential model is trained over the word-level output of the two other models combined with various engineered features [Martins et al., 2017a] on QE datasets. The linear model is the one which produces the final word-level quality labels. To obtain a final sentence-level quality estimate, the TER score produced by the APE-based model with the proportion of "BAD" labels produced by the RNN model is simply averaged.

The overall approach relies on a stacking technique to combine the neural and non-neural models. This stacking technique makes the models very flexible since any system's prediction (neural, non-neural, APE-based) can be incorporated as additional features in the linear model.

The proposed approach is compared to the highest performing word- and sentence-level QE approaches submitted to WMT15 and WMT16. For word-level QE an F-mult performance gain of 3.96% is obtained over the best WMT15 system, and 7.95% over the best WMT16 system. Results for sentence-level QE are also very positive: Pearson's r gains of 5.08% and 13.36% are obtained over the best WMT15 and WMT16 systems. A modified version of the Martins et al. [2017a] approach was also submitted to WMT17 by Martins et al. [2017b]. The main difference between the Martins et al. [2017a] and Martins et al. [2017b] approaches is that Martins et al. [2017b] use an ensemble of five sequential RNN models rather than just

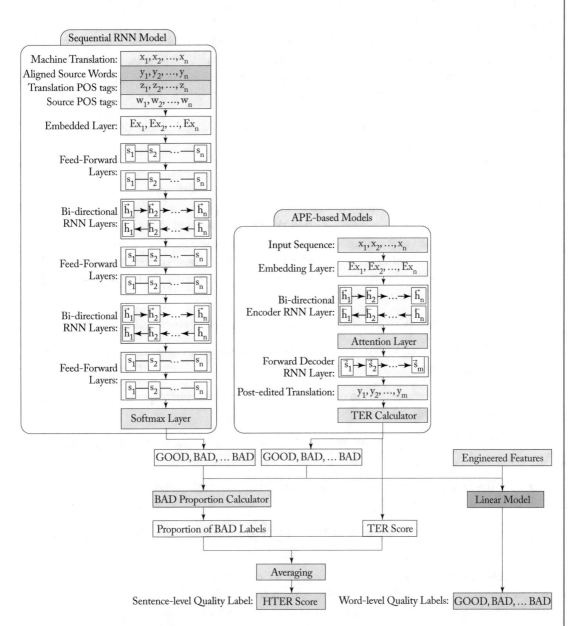

Figure 2.18: **Architecture of the** Martins et al. [2017a] **hybrid approach.**

two. Using this modified version, the Martins et al. [2017b] system achieved second place in the English-German and German-English word-level QE shared tasks of WMT17, being outperformed only by the predictor-estimators of Kim et al. [2017a].

The experiments highlight that the output of the APE-based model is a great complement to the other features used by the sequential linear model, yielding a noticeable performance increase. This observation further highlights the importance of pairing models trained over manually produced QE data with models trained with other, more abundant data. The main disadvantage of the Martins et al. [2017a] approach is the fact that it requires combining three systems in a relatively complex architecture, which may make reproducing it difficult.

2.7.3 THE APE-BASED APPROACH

Hokamp [2017] introduces a word-level QE approach whose performance is not significantly different from that of the predictor-estimator and hybrid approaches by Kim et al. [2017b] and Martins et al. [2017a] for the English-German WMT17 word-level shared task. It is a sequential APE-based approach that expands on the architecture introduced by Martins et al. [2017a] by using a larger ensemble of different encoder-decoder neural post-editing models to produce word-level predictions, as discussed in Section 2.5. All neural models use the architecture illustrated in Figure 2.19. The main components of the model are as follows.

- $\mathbf{x} = (x_1, x_2, ..., x_n)$: A sequence of n one-hot vectors that describe an input sequence.

- $E x_j$: The embedding vector of the jth element in the input sequence $\mathbf{x}$, produced by an embedding layer.

- $h_j^{\rightarrow}$: The hidden representation of the jth element in the input sequence $\mathbf{x}$, produced by a forward RNN layer.

- $h_j^{\leftarrow}$: The hidden representation of the jth element in the input sequence $\mathbf{x}$, produced by a backward RNN layer.

- $s_j^{\rightarrow}$: The hidden representation of the jth word in the machine translation $\mathbf{y}$, produced by a forward RNN layer.

- $\mathbf{y} = (y_1, y_2, ..., y_m)$: A sequence of m one-hot vectors that describe the output post-edited translation.

These models take as input a sequence that describes some type of information about the machine translation in question, which is then encoded by a bi-directional RNN layer. The encoding is then passed onto an attention layer, and then a forward RNN layer decodes a post-edited version of the machine translation. The multiple models use different kinds of inputs.

- **SRC→PE**: The input sequence is the source sentence.

- **MT→PE**: The input sequence is the translation.

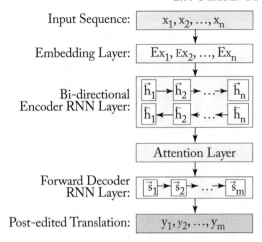

Figure 2.19: Architecture of the APE-based models used by Hokamp [2017]. They train and combine multiple models with this architecture using different types of input sequences.

- **MT-aligned→PE:** The input sequence is a modified version of the the translation where each word is concatenated with the word in the source sentence aligned to it. The word alignments are extracted from the attention layer of the SRC→PE model. If a word in the machine translation is not aligned to any word in the source sentence, then it is included on its own in the input sequence.

- **SRC+MT→PE:** The input sequence is the source sentence concatenated with the machine translation by a special BREAK marker.

- **SRC+MT-factored→PE:** The input sequence is a modified version of the sequence of the SRC+MT→PE model where each word in both the source sentence and the machine translation is concatenated with its POS tag, the dependency relation with its head word according to a dependency parse, as well as the POS tag of the head word.

Hokamp [2017] provides examples that clarify the differences between these input sequences. These examples are replicate in Table 2.2, which are given for the English source sentence "*auto vector masks apply predefined patterns as vector masks to bitmap and vector objects*" and its German machine translation "*automatische Vektor-masken vordefinierten Mustern wie Vektor-masken, Bitmaps und Vektor-objekte anwenden*".

In order to train these five models, they use a set of 500,000 artificial post-edits created by Junczys-Dowmunt and Grundkiewicz [2016]. To create this corpus, Junczys-Dowmunt and Grundkiewicz [2016] took a corpus of source English sentences and their German reference translations (an abundant resource), and applied an MT system to translate the references back into English. Then an MT system was applied again to translate the sentences back into German.

Table 2.2: Examples of the input sequences used by model variants in Hokamp [2017]. "BREAK" tokens represent a marker used by the authors to indicate a sentence split.

Model	Input Sequence
SEC	Auto vector masks apply predefined patterns as vector masks to bitmap and vector objects .
MT	Automatische Vektor- masken vordefinierten Mustern wie Vektor- masken , Bitmaps und Vektor- objekte anwenden .
MT→Aligned	automatische|auto Vektor-|vector masken|masks vordefinierten|apply Mustern|patterns wie|as Vektor-|vector masken|masks ,|to Bitmaps|to und|and Vektor-|vector objekte|objects anwenden|apply .|.
SRC+MT	Auto vector masks apply predefined patterns as vector masks to bitmap and vector objects . BREAK automatische Vektor- masken vordefinierten Mustern wie Vektor- masken , Bitmaps und Vektor- objekte anwenden .
SRC+MT→Factored	Auto|JJ|amod|NNS vector|NN|compound|NNS masks|NNS|nsub-j|VBP apply|VBP|ROOT|VBP predefined|VBN|amod|NNS patterns|NNS|dobj|VBP as|IN|prep|NNS vector|NN|compound|NNS masks|NNS|pobj|IN to|TO|aux|VB bitmap|VB|relcl|NNS and|CC|cc|VB vector|NN|compound|NNS objects|NNS|conj|VB .|.|.punct|VBP BREAK|BREAK|BREAK|BREAK Automatische|-ADJA|nk|NN Vektor-|B-NN|B-sb|B-VVINF masken|I-NN|I-sb|I-VVINF vordefinierten|ADJA|nk|NN Mustern|NN|pd|NN wie|KOKOM|cd|NN Vektor-|B-NN|B-cj|B-KOKOM masken|I-NN|I-cj|I-KOKOM ,|,|punctjNN Bitmaps|NN|cj|NN und|KON|c-d|NN Vektor-|B-NN|B-cj|B-KON objekte|I-NN|I-cj|I-KON anwen-den|VVINF|ROOT|VVINF .|.|punct|VVINF

The goal was to use the automatically produced German sentence as machine translations and the German reference as its "post-edited" version. The corpus was then complemented by "up-sampling" 20 times (i.e., creating 20 copies of) the data provided for the WMT17 English-German APE shared task (the same sentences as those in the QE word-level task). The instances in this dataset are composed of a source sentence, its machine translation, and a post-edited version of this translation. The data was up-sampled because it contains only 11,000 instances, too few compared to the 500,000 artificially produced ones.

During the training procedure, different versions of each model are kept. Once the training of a given model is concluded, the final version of this model is created by averaging the parameter values of the four highest performing kept versions. These final versions are then combined by taking a weighted average of their output. These weights are fine-tuned using the WMT17 English-German word-level shared task data with respect to F-mult.

Although this APE-based approach uses a different strategy from that used by predictor-estimator approach, they share a very important characteristic: Both use the manually produced QE data in a "supporting role". Kim et al. [2017b] train the word predictor model on raw parallel text to produce the feature vectors used as input by an estimator trained on QE data. Hokamp [2017] creates large amounts of artificial post-edits in a cost-effective way, then uses these to train APE systems that are only fine tuned over QE data.

Another interesting aspect of this approach is that it does rely on linguistic information other than just the words themselves: The SRC+MT→factored model requires POS tagging and dependency parsing for both the source and target language.

CHAPTER 3

Quality Estimation for MT at Sentence Level

3.1 INTRODUCTION

QE for MT is inspired by work on ASR (see Section 2.1), which is done at the word level. However, most work in QE to date has focused on sentence-level prediction. The motivation for sentence-level prediction is two-fold. First, MT systems generally process one sentence at a time. Even though the current state-of-the-art neural approaches to MT produce translations one word at a time, they still take as input the entire source sentence and produce as output a target sentence. Therefore, this is a rather natural unit for QE. Second, readers and other applications are very likely to consume translations one sentence at a time, or even larger chunks of text in some cases (see Chapter 4).

In sentence-level QE we are interested in producing a score that reflects the quality of an entire sentence translation. Depending on the application at hand, this score would vary but generally speaking it would be more than the simple aggregation of scores for the individual words in the sentence. Consider the example in Table 3.1, with a source (SRC) Portuguese (PT) sentence and its translation (MT) to English (EN), produced by Google Translate, and the minimally post-edited (correct) version of this translation (PE). In this example the translation has many issues with meaning preservation and disfluencies, but these are not very localized, i.e., they involve several words and ordering discrepancies, as evidenced by the comparison between the MT and PE versions.

Humans can score a sentence translation differently depending on whether it is meant for *gisting* purposes (fluency is less critical), for post-editing (some errors are easier to fix), for publication (both fluency—i.e., how well the translation reads in the target language—and adequacy—i.e., how faithful the meaning of the translation is to the source sentence—are important), to be read by someone who cannot speak the source language (adequacy is very critical), etc. Similarly, we aim to build models to predict a score that represents a specific interpretation of sentence-level quality, as indicated in the training data. This interpretation is strongly connected to the application intended for the sentence-level QE model (Section 3.2).

To build QE models we require a number of examples of source-MT sentence pairs. The number will vary depending on the ML algorithm used and how carefully the data is selected [Beck et al., 2013b], but the general rule is that at least a few thousand examples are needed, with better models built by using larger numbers of data points. Each data point is an-

Table 3.1: Example of sentence translation from Portuguese to English with various errors (in italics)

SRC (PT)	Em alguns casos, bolsas de tutoria foram concedidas para pessoas sem qualquer vínculo com as atividades de magistério, "inclusive parentes de professores que integravam o programa receberam, a título de bolsas, quantias expressivas, além disto também foram identicados casos de direcionamento de licitação com o emprego de empresas de fachada na produção de falsas cotações de preços de serviços, especialmente para a locação de veículos".
MT (EN)	In some cases, tutoring scholarships were awarded to people with no connection to teaching activities, "*including teachers' relatives who received the program received scholarships, expressive amounts, and also identified cases of bidding with the use of façade companies in the production of false prices of service prices*, especially for the leasing of vehicles."
PE (EN)	In some cases, tutoring scholarships were awarded to people with no connection to teaching activities, "in fact relatives of teachers who were part of the program received expressive amounts of money as scholarships; in addition, cases of bidding with the use of façade companies to produce false quotes for service prices, especially for the leasing of vehicles, were also identified"

notated, ideally by humans, with a quality score (Section 3.3). Given such examples, traditional approaches extract a number of features using dedicated feature extractors (Section 3.4), while neural approaches induce representations as part of the process of model building. These representations replace features extracted explicitly. Different algorithms and architectures are then used to learn a prediction model from pairs of labels and feature sets per data point (Section 3.5). Depending on the labels and algorithms used, different metrics and methods are commonly used to intrinsically and extrinsically evaluate the performance of the resulting models (Section 3.6).

The first significant effort toward sentence-level QE is reported by Blatz et al. [2003, 2004]. A large number of source, target and MT system features are used to train ML algorithms to estimate automatic metrics such as NIST [Martin and Przybocki, 2003], which are then thresholded into binary scores to distinguish "good" from "bad" translations, before or after prediction. The results were not very encouraging, possibly due to the fact that the automatic metrics used do not correlate well with human judgements at the sentence level. It may be also be the case that translations produced by MT systems at the time were too homogeneous in terms of quality: Most translations would probably be considered low quality by humans. Quirk [2004] shows that using a small set of translations manually labeled for quality makes it possible to obtain classifiers that outperform those trained on a larger set of automatically labeled translations. Specia et al. [2009a] use similar features to those in Blatz et al. [2003, 2004] to train regression algorithms on larger datasets annotated by humans for post-editing effort, rather than for "general quality". This is a much more objective notion of quality, and has become the most predominantly used label in sentence-level QE since then, as discussed in the remainder of this chapter. Much progress has been made in the past decade or so, with many new approaches emerging that predict this label type (Section 3.7).

In what follows, we describe the various aspects of sentence-level QE: Their applications (Section 3.2), quality labels (Section 3.3) and features used for training (Section 3.4), architectures (Section 3.5), evaluation methods (Section 3.6) and state-of-the-art approaches (Section 3.7).

3.2   APPLICATIONS

Work on sentence-level QE started with a focus on general quality scores—such as automatic metrics like BLEU (BiLingual Evaluation Understudy) [Papineni et al., 2002]—for tasks like n-best list reordering [Blatz et al., 2003]. This is a very intuitive application: Given a list of top translation candidates from an MT system for each source sentence that can be as large as 1,000 or 10,000 translations (depending on whether such a large number of distinct candidates can be produced), the task is to rescore these translations using information that complements that of the MT system, such that the order of candidates may change. In other words, translations with higher quality may be scored higher and moved to the top of the list. The final translation for each source sentence is chosen to be its (possibly reordered) one-best translation. N-best rescoring is a common technique in MT, where many have proposed reordering according to additional features that are only feasible or cheaper to compute after decoding is done [Och et al., 2004]. The combination of the scores from these additional features with the overall MT model score is normally done using reference translations. In QE-based rescoring, the predicted quality is used for rescoring, either individually or in combination with other scores. Despite being intuitive, this is a hard task for QE, since the translation candidates can be very similar to each other (in SMT), or so distinct from each other that comparing their predicted quality is hard (in NMT). Therefore, only marginal gains have been reported when using this technique. QE has also been used in the context of rescoring translations for spoken language translation [Ng et al., 2015a,b, 2016]. In this case, the baseline approach follows a pipeline of two modules: an ASR system followed by an MT system that takes the one-best output of the ASR system and translates it. QE-based rescoring, on the other hand, takes multiple outputs from the ASR system for each audio utterance (which in this case roughly corresponded to a sentence), translates them all, and selects the most promising one according to its estimated translation quality. The QE module uses a combination of MT and ASR features. This re-scoring approach leads to significant gains in final translation quality.

Applications targeted directly at end-users have dominated most research in QE, mainly with the goal of supporting translators in the process of post-editing MT output [Bojar et al.,

2013, 2017, 2016, 2015, Callison-Burch et al., 2012, He et al., 2010, Specia, 2011, Specia and Farzindar, 2010]. Post-editing is the task of checking and, when necessary, correcting machine translations. Even though methods for APE exist (we refer the reader to the WMT APE shared task [Bojar et al., 2017, 2016, 2015]), in the context of QE we assume human post-editing, since the quality labels need to be reliable. In production workflows, this is common practice, given that it has been shown that correcting a machine translated text is faster and cheaper than translating it from scratch [Plitt and Masselot, 2010]. However, while on average post-editing MT is faster than translating from scratch, this is not the case for all sentences. Some sentences have such low a translation quality or are so complex to fix that reading, understanding, and correcting them is more time-consuming than translating them from scratch. Therefore, estimating post-editing effort to support the work of translators is a desirable feature in computer-aided human translation workflows. QE can be framed as either a binary indicator (Is it worth post-editing a translated sentence?) or a quantifier (How much effort would be involved in fixing a translated sentence?).

The first positive results in this direction are reported in Specia et al. [2009a], where regressors are trained to predict post-editing effort on a 1–4-point scale. Subsequently, Specia et al. [2009b] use a technique to allow the automatic identification of a threshold to map a continuous predicted score (based on human annotation) to "good" and "bad" categories for filtering out low-quality translations. This threshold can be defined according to the expected confidence level of the QE model. Instead of a *Likert*-point scale, Specia and Farzindar [2010] use TER [Snover et al., 2010] to estimate the distance between machine translations and their post-edited versions (i.e., HTER [Snover et al., 2006]). The estimated scores have been shown to correlate well with human post-editing effort. However, no extrinsic evaluation with human translators is given in any of these approaches. Specia [2011] focuses on HTER and other more objective types of post-editing based annotations, such as post-editing time, and propose an extrinsic evaluation for the resulting QE models. Post-editing time is shown to be the most useful label to rank translations according to the post-editing effort they require. Specia [2011] shows that, given a fixed amount of time, human translators can correct many more words in sentences ranked by predicted post-editing time (shortest time first) than in sentences taken at random.

He et al. [2010] suggest using QE to recommend translations to post-edit from either an MT or a Translation Memory (TM) system for each source sentence. The QE model was trained on automatic annotation for TER against reference translations and the goal was to predict the translation that would yield the minimum edit distance to a reference translation. At training time this information is used to annotate sentences with a binary score indicating the system with the lowest TER (MT or Translation Memory (TM)). A classifier is then trained to recommend the MT or TM for each new source segment. Promising results have also been shown when using the estimated scores for the selection of the best translation among alternatives from different MT systems, using either individual QE models, i.e., one per MT system [Specia et al., 2010], or combined QE models, for example through multi-task learning [Shah and Specia, 2014].

Turchi et al. [2013] focus on including QE in a CAT (Computer-Aided Translation) framework. Binary classifiers ("good"—suitable for post-editing vs. "bad"—useless for post-editing) learned over training data labeled for post-editing effort (e.g., HTER), that was binarized using different ways of setting thresholds (see Section 3.3), are proposed.

Turchi et al. [2014] evaluate the empirically established thresholds with human post-editors. By comparing the time that the post-editors took to post-edit vs. the time they spent translating from scratch, individual thresholds for each post-editor are drawn. The range is [0.36–0.42] HTER, which is in line with the threshold proposed for binarizing the scores (0.40). Finally, Turchi et al. [2015] present a deeper analysis of QE as part of a CAT environment using the same 0.4 threshold over HTER to distinguish "bad" from "good" machine translations. In order to inform post-editors about the quality of machine translated sentences, each sentence received a color (green for "good" and red for "bad"). The color-coded machine translations were compared against a control group in terms of post-editing time. No strong differences between the two settings were found. However, when analyzing individual segments, in around 51% of the segments post-editors were found to be faster when they were given information about the quality of the MT output. Turchi et al. [2015] suggest that segments with $0.2 < \text{HTER} \leq 0.5$ would benefit more from having color-coded translations than segments in other HTER intervals.

In a more recent study, Parra Escartín et al. [2017] simulate a similar production workflow with post-editors informed on translation quality using QE scores. Following Turchi et al. [2015], a "traffic light" scheme is proposed for showing the quality of a machine translation for the post-editors.

- **Yellow:** The post-editor should translate the sentence from scratch, i.e., no machine translation is given.

- **Blue:** The machine translation is given to the post-editor, but no information about its quality is revealed, i.e., QE is not used.

- **Green:** The machine translation is given to the post-editor, with a hint that the QE system suggests that it should be post-edited.

- **Red:** The machine translation is given to the post-editor, but with a hint that the QE system suggests that is should be translated from scratch.

Instead of predicting HTER, Parra Escartín et al. [2017] use the target-side Fuzzy Match Score (FMS), i.e., the FMS score between the machine translation and the post-edited version, as quality labels for QE. FMS is a concept borrowed from translation memories that measures the percentage of character or word changes needed between a translation found for a given new source sentence and the closest matching sentence in a database of previously collected translations (i.e., a TM). For the color scheme, sentences scoring 75% or higher were considered worth post-editing (green). In order to evaluate the impact of QE on translator productivity, portions of the data were selected where the QE system performed well (small difference between predicted FMS and true FMS), and segments where QE performed poorly. Four post-editors were asked to perform the task with the "traffic light" approach. Parra Escartín et al. [2017] report that when faced with accurate QE predictions the productivity of post-editors improves. Post-editors are faster when editing sentences predicted as good.

Other potential applications for sentence-level QE include making a decision on whether or not a translation can be published as is. For example, social media platforms used by native speakers of multiple languages to communicate, can use MT to translate posts and show them directly in the native language of the user. However, if the translation is predicted to be unreliable, it would be better to show the post in its original language and offer MT as optional (potentially with a disclaimer). The application, in this case, is *gisting*, and the challenge is to make sure the translation is comprehensible and not misleading. This applies to a wide range of content types where the question is whether or not to publish or use the translation as is, but more often this decision is taken at the entire text level, such as with e-mails and other internal communication, product descriptions and reviews on e-commerce platforms, and any other online content. Along this line of application, Turchi et al. [2012] use QE at sentence level and metrics for sentence informativeness within a document in order to rank machine-translated sentences according to their quality and relevance.

3.3   LABELS

As mentioned earlier, the first type of label for sentence-level QE was computed automatically based on reference translations. Blatz et al. [2003, 2004] attempt to use these metric scores directly to predict a continuous score between 0 and 1, which is then thresholded to obtain a "good" vs. "bad" final decision. This has proved to be a hard problem given the low reliability of MT evaluation metrics. To remedy this issue, the metric scores are then first discretized into two classes: the top 5% or 30% of all translations according to a given metric are considered good quality, while the remaining, bad quality. The 5%/30% thresholds are defined in somewhat arbitrary ways.

Gamon et al. [2005] propose a way to automatically label sentences with "good"/"bad" labels by collecting a mix of human and machine translations and labeling the former as "bad" and while the latter as "good". The task becomes then to distinguish human from machine translations, which perhaps at the time was a fair proxy to distinguishing good from bad translations. Nowadays, however, we know that machine translations for certain types of texts can have the same level of quality as one would expect from humans. In other words, low human-likeness does not necessarily imply low MT quality.

Quirk [2004] was the first to introduce the use of manually assigned labels to sentences. The labels vary from 1–4, with meanings as follows.

- **1 - Unacceptable:** Absolutely incomprehensible and/or little or no information transferred accurately.

- **2 - Possibly Acceptable:** Possibly comprehensible (given enough context and/or time to work it out); some information transferred accurately.

- **3 - Acceptable:** Not perfect (stylistically or grammatically odd), but definitely comprehensible, and with accurate transfer of all important information.

- **4 - Ideal:** Not necessarily a perfect translation, but grammatically correct, and with all information accurately transferred.

Each sentence was judged by six human annotators and the scores were averaged. Results on a small set of 350 sentences proved much better than those obtained using automatic annotations on a much larger set of instances, motivating most subsequent work in QE. A similar 1–4-point scale also focusing on the adequacy of the translations is used in Specia et al. [2011], where these scores are also converted into binary classes through different groupings: "adequate" (scores 3 and 4, i.e., same or very similar meaning to the source sentence) vs. "inadequate" (scores 1 and 2, i.e., different meaning than that of the source sentence) translations or "fully adequate" (score 4) from "partially adequate or inadequate" (scores 1, 2, and 3) translations.

As part of the annual WMT evaluation campaigns between 2007 and 2016, translations produced by different MT systems have been ranked by humans using a 5-way ranking (i.e., 5 different MT systems sampled at a time). Given the availability of this data, some research has addressed QE as a ranking task, generally converting the rankings into pairwise ranks first [Avramidis, 2012, 2013].

Using the same WMT data, system ranking was also explored as a quality label for the WMT13 QE shared task [Bojar et al., 2013]. Participants were asked to predict the order for individual pairs of translations provided by different MT systems.

In addition to ranking across MT systems, a variant that has also been explored in all editions of WMT QE shared tasks is the task of ranking sentences produced by the same MT system: The idea is to predict the position of a sentence in relation to all the other sentences in the test set. In the WMT tasks, the gold sentence rankings are obtained by sorting sentences according to their scoring labels, while system rankings can be generated in any way using whatever type of label participants choose.

More recently, sentence-level QE has been exploring various types of discrete and continuous post-editing effort labels. According to Krings [2001], post-editing effort has three dimensions: temporal, cognitive, and technical. The temporal dimension is the measurement of the time spent by the post-editor to transform the MT output into a good-quality post-edited version. Although cognitive aspects are directly related to temporal effort, they cannot be fully captured by time. Cognitive aspects encompass various linguistic phenomena and style patterns, and they can only be measured by indirect means of effort assessment (e.g., keystrokes, pauses). Finally, the technical dimension involves the practical transformations performed in order to achieve the post-edited version. Such transformations can be insertions, deletions, movements, or a combination of these. The technical dimension focuses on the different operations without accounting for the complexity of such operations as a function of linguistic properties of the text as it is done in the cognitive dimension.

The most intuitive and direct measure of post-editing effort is post-editing time. The (normalized) time taken to post-edit can be used as a proxy for quality: Segments that take longer to be post-edited are considered worse than segments that can be quickly corrected. Koponen et al. [2012] argue that post-editing time is the most effective way of measuring cognitive aspects of the post-editing task and relating them to the quality of the machine translations. Such a quality label was used in WMT13 and WMT14 QE shared tasks [Bojar et al., 2013, 2014].

Post-editing time can, however, be inaccurate and difficult to use in practice. First, it is subject to outliers, since translators can get distracted or take breaks while translating a sentence. Second, a high variation among different translators' post-editing times is expected, given that translators have different typing skills, translation experience, and proficiency with the post-editing tool, among other aspects. Finally, post-editing time can encompass reading time, correction time and revision time, and the relationship between these factors is unclear.

Perceived post-editing effort is an alternative way of evaluating post-editing effort and it has been generally used in an attempt to capture cognitive effort. In this evaluation approach, humans are asked to give a score for the machine translated sentences according to a *Likert* scale [Specia, 2011]. This type of score can be given with or without actual post-editing and they represent the human's belief on the degree of difficulty to fix the given machine translated sentences. In the first and second editions of the WMT QE shared task [Bojar et al., 2013, Callison-Burch et al., 2012], the *Likert* scale varied from 1 to 5 as follows:

- **1:** The MT output is incomprehensible, with little or no information transferred accurately. It cannot be edited and must be translated from scratch.

- **2:** About 50–70% of the MT output needs to be edited. It requires significant editing effort in order to reach publishable level.

- **3:** About 25–50% of the MT output needs to be edited. It contains different errors and mistranslations that need to be corrected.

- **4:** About 10–25% of the MT output needs to be edited. It is generally clear and intelligible.

- **5:** The MT output is perfectly clear and intelligible. It is not necessarily a perfect translation, but requires little to no editing.

For WMT14 the post-editing effort task was based on the following *Likert* scale [Bojar et al., 2014].

- **1 - Perfect translation**: No post-editing needed at all.

- **2 - Near miss translation:** Translation contains no more than three errors, and possibly additional errors that can be easily fixed (capitalization, punctuation).

- **3 - Very low-quality translation:** Cannot be easily fixed.

Even though cognitive effort is an important dimension of the post-editing process, its measurement is usually expensive and unreliable. Perceived post-editing effort can be highly influenced by differences in the view of annotators and how accepting of MT they are.

Finally, post-editing effort can also be evaluated indirectly by using a metric that takes into account **edit operations** (technical effort). HTER is an example of such a metric. HTER compares a post-edited machine translation to the original machine translation using TER, and computes the minimum number of edits to transform the machine translation into the post-edited version. HTER is the most widely used quality label for QE, having featured in all editions of WMT since 2013 [Bojar et al., 2013, 2014, 2017, 2016, 2015] and is usually capped such that it is between 0 and 1.

Turchi et al. [2014] argue that the notion of MT quality is inherently subjective, and relying on continuous scores such as HTER might result in unreliable or uninformative annotations. An automatic method to obtain binary annotated data that explicitly discriminates between useful (suitable for post-editing) and useless translations is proposed. This method measures similarities and dissimilarities between an automatic translation (MT), its post-edited version (PE), and the corresponding reference translation (REF). The assumption is that if the MT is far from its post-edited version and also far from the reference translation, this is a strong indication that it is a low-quality MT. Turchi et al. [2014] build a classifier that learns a similarity threshold T such that: (i) a pair (MT,PE) with similarity less than or equal to T will be considered a negative example ("bad"), and (ii) a pair (MT,PE) with similarity greater than T will be considered positive ("good"). Once the dataset is annotated in such a way, a binary classifier can be used to train a prediction model for unseen source and machine translated sentences. Experiments demonstrate that this yields better models than those based on the adaptation of available QE corpora into binary datasets. Furthermore, analysis suggests that the induced thresholds separating useful from useless translations are significantly lower than those suggested in the existing guidelines for human annotators.

Finally, Parra Escartín et al. [2017] discuss the use of target-side FMS as a more adequate indicator for post-editors and, therefore, a more reliable label for QE. The argument is that post-editors are more familiar with FMS, since this is a widely used metric in the translation industry, while HTER is only used for academic purposes. The target-side FMS is calculated on the level of trigrams of characters between the machine translation and its post-edited version. FMS scores vary in [0,100] and are usually reported as percentages.

3.4   FEATURES

Significant effort in QE has been dedicated to devising and extracting features of various types to build models. One common distinction that is made among existing features is whether they are extracted from the MT system that generated the translations ("glass-box" features) or independently from this MT system ("black-box" features). The former type is also referred to as "confidence" features. Extractors can rely on the source sentence, its machine translation, and a number of external resources, such as the parallel corpus used to train the MT system, or larger parallel corpora or corpora of the source or target language. Linguistic tools such as parsers or even other MT systems can also be used. In Figure 3.1 we categorize different types of features in four groups, depending on whether they process the source or target sentences, or both, and whether they use MT-system specific information. We describe and exemplify each of these categories in what follows, as well as discuss other features that fall outside these main groups. The list we give for each category comprises examples of commonly used sentence-level features and is not meant to be exhaustive.

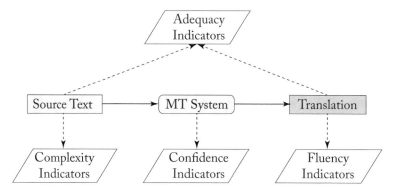

Figure 3.1: Categories of features for QE.

3.4.1 COMPLEXITY FEATURES

Complexity features reflect how difficult it is to translate the source text. The harder it is to translate a sentence, the higher the chances of its quality being low. They are extracted from the source sentence only:

- source sentence length;

- source sentence type/token ratio;

- source sentence trigram LM (language model) probability obtained based on a large in-domain corpus of the source language;

- percentage of unigrams to trigrams in the source sentence belonging to each frequency quartile of the source corpus;

- percentage of distinct uni to trigrams seen in the source corpus;

- average frequency of source words in the source corpus;

- width of parse tree of source sentence;

- maximum/average source parse tree depth;

- number of relative/attributive clauses in source sentence;

- average number of translations per source sentence word, as given by probabilistic dictionaries;

- partial source trees represented using tree kernels;

- existence of URL address in the source sentence; and

- features based on composition of word embeddings for the source sentence.

3.4.2   FLUENCY FEATURES

Fluency features attempt to measure how natural, fluent, and grammatical the translation is. They are extracted from the target sentence only:

- target sentence trigram LM probability obtained based on a large in-domain corpus of the target language, or web-scaled LM features;

- % of 1–5-grams that appear in a target LM at least once;

- target sentence length;

- target sentence type/token ratio;

- average number of occurrences of each target word within the target sentence;

- target sentence trigram LM probability trained on a POS-tags version of a large in-domain corpus of the target language;

- number of mismatching opening/closing brackets and quotation marks in the target sentence;

- coherence of the target sentence using entity-grid models such as Burstein et al. [2010];

- number of subjects in target sentence;

- whether or not the target sentence begins with a verb;

- partial target trees represented using tree kernels;

- number of untranslated words;

- features based on composition of word embeddings for the target sentence; and

- grammaticality of the sentence using grammar checking tools.

3.4.3 CONFIDENCE FEATURES

Most initial work focused on confidence features. These reflect how confident the MT system is about the produced translation, such as the internal model component scores in SMT systems. They are extracted from the MT system:

- global score of the MT system for the translation;

- if using SMT, internal features of the system, such as phrase probability;

- number of translation hypotheses in the n-best list;

- proportion of out-of-vocabulary words;

- uni to trigram LM probability using translations in the n-best as LM;

- relative frequency of the words in the translation in the n-best list;

- ratio of MT model score of the top translation to the sum of the scores of all hypotheses in the n-best list;

- average size of hypotheses in the n-best list;

- n-best list density (vocabulary size/average sentence length);

- edit distance of the current hypothesis to the centroid hypothesis; and

- if using a search graph in SMT style, total of hypotheses in the search graph, proportion of discarded/pruned/recombined graph nodes.

3.4.4 ADEQUACY FEATURES

Adequacy features attempt to capture how close or related the source and translation sentences are on different linguistic levels. This is the most difficult type of feature to reliably extract since the source and target sentences are in different languages. They are extracted from both the source and target sentences:

- ratio of number of tokens in source and target sentences;

- bilingual word embedding models to measure the similarity between the source and target sentences using their compositional vector representations;

- alignment features: e.g., mean number of alignments for each source word, maximum number of alignments for each source word, number of unaligned words in target sentence;

- ratio of percentages of numbers, content-/non-content words in the source and target sentences;

- ratio of percentage of nouns/verbs/pronouns/etc. in the source and target sentences;

- absolute difference between number of superficial constructions in the source and target sentences: brackets, numbers, punctuation marks;

- proportion of dependency relations with constituents aligned between source and target sentences;

- difference between the depth of the syntactic trees of the source and target sentences;

- difference between the number of PP/NP/VP/ADJP/ADVP/CONJP phrases in the source and target sentences;

- difference between the number of person/location/organization entities in source and target sentences; and

- proportion of matching chunk labels in the source and target sentences.

3.4.5   PSEUDO-REFERENCE AND BACK-TRANSLATION FEATURES

A family of features that has been extensively explored and can be somewhat categorized as confidence features are those based on so-called "pseudo-references". Initially proposed by Albrecht and Hwa [2008] as a proxy to using human references for traditional MT evaluation, pseudo-references are machine translations produced by an MT system other than the one we want to predict the quality for. Once such pseudo-references are available (one or more, from one of more MT systems), different metrics of similarity between the pseudo-reference and the output of the MT system of interest can be computed. These include standard evaluation metrics such as BLEU, TER, etc., or any type of string similarity metric. The scores of these metrics are often then used as features to complement other feature sets. The intuition is that if two or more independent systems lead to similar translations, there is a higher chance that the translation is correct. This works as a "consensus" indicator, but it can of course be misleading if the MT systems used follow very similar approaches and/or are built from the same training data, which would make them more likely to produce similar translations, regardless of their quality. Another interpretation is that if an independent MT system is known to be consistently better (or worse) than the MT system of interest, similarity (or dissimilarity) to the translations produced by such a system would indicate high (or low) quality.

A related type of feature is based on back-translations: The sentence translation is back-translated to the source language (using the same or another MT system) and metrics of string similarity between source sentence and a back-translated version of a machine translated sentence can be used as features. The intuition is that if the source sentence can be reconstructed from its machine translated version, the quality of the translation is high. This, however, can be misleading as any dissimilarities to the source sentence could be because of the MT system used for the back-translation rather than the system used for the forward translation.

3.4.6   LINGUISTICALLY MOTIVATED FEATURES

A popular direction in QE until recently was the design of linguistically motivated, often language-specific features. For example, Felice and Specia [2012] propose and study many of the features described above through ablation tests. Through feature selection, linguistically motivated features make up 40% of the features selected as best. Kozlova et al. [2016] study the contribution of a number of more traditional syntactic features over parse trees of source and target sentences, such as width (number of dependencies from root node), maximum depth, proportion of internal nodes, number of subjects, relative clauses, etc. These include examples of language specific, linguistically motivated features, such as whether the German polite imperative is used as a translation for the simple English imperative in QE for English-German MT. Overall, previous work has shown the potential of linguistic features for the task.

Given the large number and variety of features and often relatively small training sets, performing feature selection is a very common practice and has proved beneficial. Many techniques based on forward and backward selection have been used. Shah et al. [2015a] use Gaussian processes (GPs) as an efficient technique to understand the contribution of larger feature sets on the performance of prediction models.

Explicit features such as the ones described here have also been combined with representations learned from data using word or sentence embeddings [Martins et al., 2017b, Shah et al., 2016, 2015b], or in some cases even replaced entirely by such representations for the source or target languages [Kim et al., 2017b, Paetzold and Specia, 2016a] or bilingually [Abdelsalam et al., 2016], as we will discuss in Section 3.7.

A final popular direction when it comes to features is the use of multi-level prediction models, where predictions made by lower-level QE systems can be used directly as features, such as the proportion of words (or specific types of words, e.g., as content words) that are predicted as "bad" by a word-level QE system or length of the longest sequence of "good" or "bad" word predictions [Camargo de Souza et al., 2014, Tezcan et al., 2016], or indirectly in inherently multi-level approaches [Kim et al., 2017b, Martins et al., 2017b].

3.5   ARCHITECTURES

The main architectures for sentence-level QE revolve around classification and regression algorithms. For labels represented as continuous scores (e.g., HTER, post-editing time, BLEU), regression algorithms are the natural choice. The most popular algorithms used for that are[1] naive Bayes [Blatz et al., 2004], linear regression [Quirk, 2004, Tezcan et al., 2016], SVM [Felice and Specia, 2012, Langlois et al., 2012, Specia et al., 2010], partial least squares [Specia et al., 2009a], M5P [Soricut et al., 2012], SVM with tree kernels [Hardmeier et al., 2012], single- and multi-layer perceptron [Blatz et al., 2004, Buck, 2012, Hildebrand and Vogel, 2013], random forests [Tezcan et al., 2016], extremely randomized trees [Camargo de Souza et al., 2013],

---

[1]Note that we only provide a few examples of early work that used certain learning algorithms, many more examples can be found in the WMT reports.

GPs [Beck et al., 2013a, Cohn and Specia, 2013], ridge regression [Biçici and Way, 2014], RNNs [Kim and Lee, 2016, Kim et al., 2017b, Paetzold and Specia, 2016a], and SVM or GPs with multi-task learning with different types of kernels, for example tree kernels [Beck et al., 2015, Hardmeier et al., 2012]. It is also common to ensemble models; for example Martins et al. [2017a] combine a linear feature-based classifier with a neural network. Multi-level prediction methods have also been proposed that perform word-level QE and use the proportion of words predicted as "bad" as HTER scores, or that use the HTER between the machine translation and the output of an automatic post-editing system on that machine-translated sentence [Martins et al., 2017b].

For discrete labels (e.g., binary "good"/"bad", 1–4- or 1–5-point scale), classification algorithms are the most natural choice. Popular algorithms include SVM [Turchi et al., 2014] and naive Bayes classifiers. In fact, for labels with more than two possible values, most work has used regression or ranking algorithms. When treating the task as a ranking problem, it is a common approach to decompose ranks into pairs and use classifiers for pairwise classification, such as logistic regression [Avramidis and Popovic, 2013] and random forests [Formiga et al., 2013].

The use of multiple MT systems at a time for ranking assumes the labels follow an ordinal distribution, as in Shah and Specia [2014], where the datasets contained three alternative translations produced by three different types of MT systems and the task was to select the best translations using absolute annotations that had been produced independently for each system.

3.6   EVALUATION

Sentence-level QE evaluation is strongly connected to how the training (and test) data is labeled—and therefore what type of model is built. The vast majority of work is addressed as a scoring problem, where absolute numeric labels are predicted. As previously mentioned, even though in some cases the training data is annotated with discrete (or ordinal) labels, regression algorithms are used for model building and therefore these models are evaluated as such. For the evaluation of scoring tasks, where the labels are either continuous or ordinal, automatic regression-based evaluation metrics are applied. Until 2015, Mean Absolute Error (MAE) was the primary metric used for that, with Root-Mean-Squared Error (RMSE) used as a secondary metric. MAE is calculated using Equation (3.1) where, for a given test set S, $\hat{y}_i$ is the predicted score for instance i ($1 \leq i \leq n$), y_i is the true score, and n is the number of data points in the test set. Similarly, RMSE is calculated using Equation (3.2):

$$MAE = \frac{\sum_{i=1}^{n} |\hat{y}_i - y_i|}{n} \qquad (3.1)$$

$$RMSE = \sqrt{\frac{\sum_{i=1}^{n} (\hat{y}_i - y_i)^2}{n}}. \qquad (3.2)$$

Both MAE and RMSE are nonparametric and deterministic. They can also be easily interpreted: For instance, an MAE score of 0.5 means that, on average, the difference between the predicted value and the true value is 0.5. RMSE has a similar interpretation, although it penalizes larger errors more severely [Callison-Burch et al., 2012].

As Graham [2015] points out, MAE and RMSE are not reliable for evaluating QE tasks since it is highly sensitive to variance. This means that, if the predictions of a given QE model show high variance, it will lead to a high MAE, even though the distribution of the predictions follows the distribution of the true labels. This problem is common in datasets for QE at sentence level. Graham [2015] suggests instead the use of the Pearson's r correlation coefficient as a metric for QE system evaluation, which is described in Equation (3.3). Pearson's r measures the linear correlation between two variables, which in this case are the predicted labels $\hat{y} = \{\hat{y}_1, \hat{y}_2, ..., \hat{y}_n\}$ and the human-produced labels $y = \{y_1, y_2, ..., y_n\}$ (n is the number of samples):

$$r = \frac{n\left(\sum_{i=1}^{n} \hat{y}_i y_i\right) - \left(\sum_{i=1}^{n} \hat{y}_i\right)\left(\sum_{i=1}^{n} y_i\right)}{\sqrt{\left[n\left(\sum_{i=1}^{n} \hat{y}_i^2\right) - \left(\sum_{i=1}^{n} \hat{y}_i\right)^2\right]\left[n\left(\sum_{i=1}^{n} y_i^2\right) - \left(\sum_{i=1}^{n} y_i\right)^2\right]}}. \tag{3.3}$$

Pearson's r correlation coefficient varies between -1 and 1, where -1 is the maximum value of negative correlation, while 1 is the maximum value of positive correlation, and 0 indicates no correlation at all. Most current work on sentence-level QE uses Pearson's r as the main evaluation metric, although MAE and RMSE are still used as secondary metrics, since information about the variance of the data is also important. However, as pointed out by Camargo de Souza [2016], Pearson's r is defined with four assumptions about the variables under investigation: (i) both follow a continuous distribution; (ii) there is a linear relationship between them; (iii) they both approximately follow a normal distribution; and (iv) the outliers in the data are not significant. Camargo de Souza [2016] shows, however, several cases of datasets for sentence-level QE where the quality labels are not normally distributed, which would make Pearson's r correlation coefficient less reliable. Also, there is no study of outliers in QE datasets in order to guarantee that they are not significant. Therefore, it is not clear whether or not Pearson's r is the most reliable evaluation metric for all quality labels of sentence-level QE. A recommendation is to consider both MAE and Pearson's r in combination.

For models treating discrete labels as classes, standard classification metrics such as classification accuracy, precision and recall can be used. For binary classifiers, a more informative metric is ROC curves or IROC, the integral of the curve for a single overall quantitative figure [Blatz et al., 2003, Quirk, 2004]. ROC curves plot the sensitivity (the true positive rate) against the specificity (the true negative rate) for different thresholds. A perfect classifier will have a curve that stays maximally close to the upper-left corner, where a random classifier will stay on the line from $(0, 0)$ to $(1, 1)$. An ideal classifier will have an IROC of 1, whereas a random classifier will have an IROC of 0.5.

For models performing translation ranking, DeltaAvg and Spearman's ρ rank correlation coefficient are popular metrics. DeltaAvg [Callison-Burch et al., 2012] was introduced in the context of the WMT shared tasks and was used as the primary metric until 2015. Spearman's ρ has been used as the primary metric since then because it is easier to interpret.

DeltaAvg is a useful metric to evaluate ranks derived from extrinsic metrics (e.g., ranks derived from HTER values). It measures how useful a predicted rank is according to an extrinsic quality metric. A parameterized version of DeltaAvg is defined in Equation (3.4). $DeltaAvg_V[n]$ is calculated, where $V(s)$ is the extrinsic quality label of a given sentence and $V(S)$ represents the average of all $V(s)$ in the set of sentences S ($s \in S$).[2] n is a parameter that defines the number of quantiles of equal sizes that will divide S.[3] In this case, assuming S is a set of ranked sentences, S_1, the first quantile of S, contains the highest ranked sentences, S_2 is the second quantile, and so on until S_n. Also, $S_{i,j} = \bigcup_{k=i}^{j} S_k$. Such parameterized version of DeltaAvg measures the average difference in quality of $n - 1$ cases. Each case measures the impact of adding a new quantile:

$$DeltaAvg_V[n] = \frac{\sum_{k=1}^{n-1} V(S_{1,k})}{n - 1} - V(S).$$ (3.4)

The final DeltaAvg value is defined as shown by Equation (3.5), where $N = |S|/2$. This is non-parametric and deterministic. It also has a reasonably intuitive interpretation: DeltaAvg equal to 0.5 means that, on average, the difference in quality between the top-ranked quantiles and the overall quality is 0.5:

$$DeltaAvg_V = \frac{\sum_{n=2}^{N} DeltaAvg_V[n]}{N - 1}.$$ (3.5)

Spearman's ρ is a general metric of ranking correlation. It is a nonparametric test that aims to measure to what degree the relationship between two variables can be defined as a monotonic function. Spearman's ρ is calculated using Equation (3.3), but using the ranks instead of the real values [Zwillinger and Kokoska, 1999]. Equation (3.6) shows how Spearman's ρ is calculated, where n is the number of samples, $u_{\hat{y}_i}$ is the rank for the ith instance in sample $\hat{y}$ and u_{y_i} is the rank for the $i^t h$ instance in sample y (with $n = |y| = |\hat{y}|$ and $1 \leq i \leq n$). Spearman's ρ also varies between -1 (maximum negative correlation) and 1 (maximum positive correlation):

$$\rho = \frac{n \left(\sum_{i=1}^{n} u_{\hat{y}_i} u_{y_i} \right) - \left(\sum_{i=1}^{n} u_{\hat{y}_i} \right) \left(\sum_{i=1}^{n} u_{y_i} \right)}{\sqrt{\left[n \left(\sum_{i=1}^{n} u_{\hat{y}_i}^2 \right) - \left(\sum_{i=1}^{n} u_{\hat{y}_i} \right)^2 \right] \left[n \left(\sum_{i=1}^{n} u_{y_i}^2 \right) - \left(\sum_{i=1}^{n} u_{y_i} \right)^2 \right]}}.$$ (3.6)

For pairwise ranking tasks such as the one run during WMT13, Kendall's τ correlation coefficient is used as evaluation metric. This metric compares the predicted pairwise rankings of two translations for a given source segment from different systems with the corresponding pairwise ranks given by humans. Equation (3.7) shows how this metric is calculated:

$$\tau = \frac{|\text{concordant pairs}| - |\text{discordant pairs}|}{|\text{total pairs}|},$$ (3.7)

[2]V is a function of quality, which could be HTER, post-editing effort *Likert* scores, etc.
[3]If $|S|$ is not divisible by n, S_n should contain the rest of the entries

where concordant pairs are the cases in which a system translation for a given source segment received the same rank value by both the human and the QE system, discordant pairs are the pairs for which human and QE system do not agree, and total pairs is the total number of pairs being evaluated.

The values for τ vary between -1 (all pairs are discordant pairs) and 1 (all pairs are concordant pairs). Systems with higher Kendall's τ values are expected to show higher correlation with human scores. Kendall's τ is also calculated differently according to the way that ties are treated. If ties are to be penalized, Kendall's τ will work as a recall metric where the purpose is to measure how much of the difference in quality given by a human has been captured by the predictions. On the other hand, if ties are ignored, this metric works as a precision metric, where the purpose is to evaluate to how much of the difference in predicted quality actually occurs in the human annotation.

Other metrics have been used for the extrinsic evaluation of quality predictions. Examples include overall test set performance (e.g., using metrics like BLEU) after (i) n-best list reranking based on quality predictions for candidate translations for each source sentence [Blatz et al., 2003, Quirk, 2004] or (ii) system selection, where one of many alternative translations from multiple MT systems is chosen for each source sentence [Shah and Specia, 2014], and time needed to post-edit a set of translations selected to have the highest (predicted) quality vs. a set of randomly selected translations [Specia, 2011].

3.7 STATE-OF-THE-ART RESULTS

Based on the findings of WMT shared tasks, we found that two approaches have particularly pushed the boundaries of QE in recent years: The sequential predictor-estimator neural approach of Kim et al. [2017b] for word-, phrase-, and sentence-level QE, and the hybrid sequential and automatic post-editing-based approach of Martins et al. [2017a] for word- and sentence-level QE. These contributions feature two distinct strategies with some similarities and achieved exceptional results in the WMT shared tasks of 2015, 2016, and 2017. These contributions were both described in Section 2.7, since they also perform word-level QE. For a head to head comparison with other recent approaches, we refer the reader to the report from the WMT17 shared task [Bojar et al., 2017].

As with the word-level task, in the 2017 edition of the WMT shared task, participants were encouraged to evaluate their approaches using not only the current edition's datasets, but also datasets from the previous edition. Again, the training set in 2017 is a superset of that in 2016, produced by the same MT system, for the same text domain and annotated in the same way. The top system at WMT2016 was only the fourth best compared to the WMT17 submissions. In addition, half of WMT16 participants were below the 2017 baseline system.

CHAPTER 4

Quality Estimation for MT at Document Level

4.1 INTRODUCTION

In this chapter, we present document-level QE with a focus on MT. Document-level QE [Scarton, 2015, 2017, Scarton and Specia, 2014a, Soricut and Echihabi, 2010] is the least explored of the granularity levels. Given an entire translated "document", the task consists in predicting its quality as a whole. We use the term "document" to generally refer to texts that contain multiple sentences, from short paragraphs with 3–5 sentences to long texts such as a complete news article.

Traditional MT systems process the input text sentence by sentence and are completely oblivious to document-level information. This may affect the translation of discourse elements and result in an incoherent text. Table 4.1 shows a paragraph extracted from a source text (SRC) in Portuguese (PT) and its machine-translated version in English (EN) using Google Translate. Although the machine-translated text has several problems, we will focus on the highlighted words that represent the same entity across mentions and constitute example of errors that could only be solved if the MT system used information beyond sentences. In sentence (2), the correctly translated pronoun "*she*" refers to "*housewife*" in sentence (1). In sentence (3), instead of using pronouns, the entity changes to "*the 63-year-old victim*" which should still refer to "*housewife*" in sentence (1), but is not marked for gender, as it is not necessary. However, as a consequence, the pronoun "*lhe*" in the same source sentence, which still refers to housewife, is incorrectly translated to "*him*", when it should be translated to "*her*".

Document-level QE is particularly appealing in *gisting* cases, where end users will consume the MT as is (Section 4.2). It has some practical challenges that make it harder than sentence- and word-level QE. One of the biggest challenges is the task of scoring documents according to some perceived quality scale (e.g., perceived post-editing effort or perceived adequacy). This task is expected to be even more subjective than it is for finer-grained levels. While it is straightforward for a human to score words and, in most cases sentences, according to their quality, the document-level assessment has proven to be more complex [Scarton et al., 2015b]. Annotators can be misled by errors at other levels, and the annotations may not reflect the quality of the document as a whole.

One solution for the problem of subjectivity in human annotation at document level would be to use aggregated sentence or word-level scores. However, such an approach also has flaws.

Table 4.1: Example of paragraph translation from Portuguese to English with various errors

SRC (PT)	1- **Uma dona de casa** foi vítima do golpe do bilhete premiado nesta terça-feira. 2- **Ela** perdeu R$ 5 mil. 3- De acordo com os registros policiais, após estacionar **seu** carro pela rua Enfrid Frick, no Jardim Paraíso, **a vítima** de 63 anos foi abordada por uma mulher que disse se chamar "Rosa", a qual *lhe* indagou sobre um endereço, iniciando uma conversa dizendo que procurava uma pessoa que havia oferecido R$ 20 mil por um bilhete premiado da Mega Sena.
MT (EN)	1- **A housewife** fell victim to the winning ticket on Tuesday. 2- **She** lost R$ 5 thousand. 3- According to police records, after parking **his** car down Enfrid Frick Street in Jardim Paraíso, **the 63-year-old victim** was approached by a woman who said she was called "Rosa", who asked *him* about an address, starting a conversation saying who was looking for a person who had offered R$ 20,000 for an award-winning Mega Sena ticket.
PE (EN)	1- **A housewife** fell victim to the fraudulent winning ticket this Tuesday. 2- **She** lost R$ 5 thousand. 3- According to police records, after parking **her** car down Enfrid Frick Street in Jardim Paraíso, **the 63-year-old victim** was approached by a woman who introduced herself as "Rosa", and asked *the housewife* about an address, starting a conversation saying that she was looking for a person who had offered her R$ 20,000 for a winning Mega Sena ticket.

The main motivation behind devising quality scores at document level instead of simply combining word or sentence-level scores is that some sentences can be good in isolation but inadequate when put into context. Conversely, sentences can score poorly in isolation but be considered acceptable when put into document context, e.g., in a *gisting* scenario. This behavior is expected mainly from MT approaches that translate at sentence level, disregarding any document-level context, e.g., the majority of statistical and neural MT approaches, which are trained on parallel data with shuffled sentences. Moreover, sentences can have different relevance in a document. Sentences that are more important for document comprehension are more problematic if incorrectly translated than sentences that play a less important role in the document (Section 4.3). Another solution is to rely on task-based labels, which are, however, more time-consuming and expensive. For example, the reading comprehension approach presented in Section 4.3 requires reliable questions to be devised for each document.

Another major challenge is finding data for annotation. As stated in Chapter 2, for building a QE model a few thousands annotated data points are need. However, datasets for document-level QE, when available, are much smaller. The WMT16 shared task for document-level QE [Bojar et al., 2016], for instance, made a training set with 146 documents available. The difficulties in gathering data for document-level QE are two-fold. First, the majority of parallel datasets with source-MT pairs are at the sentence level, without the possibility of recovering the documents from which the sentences were taken.

The first work on document-level QE is by Soricut and Echihabi [2010]. It explores document-level QE prediction to rank documents translated by a given MT system, predicting BLEU scores. Following this work, others focus on scoring documents according to automatic metrics [Scarton and Specia, 2014a], document-level labels devised from post-editing [Bojar et al., 2016, Scarton, 2017, Scarton et al., 2015b] and scores devised from reading comprehension tests [Scarton, 2017, Scarton and Specia, 2016]. In terms of features, architectures, and evaluation (Sections 4.4, 4.5 and 4.6, respectively), work for document-level QE primarily follows approaches developed for sentence-level. In addition, a handful of specific features have been proposed for this level of QE. The state-of-the-art solutions are very different for document-level QE, since the successful sequential multi-level approaches presented in Chapters 2 and 3 are not applicable to document-level prediction in practice.

In the remainder of this chapter, we present applications for document-level QE (Section 4.2), different types of quality labels (Section 4.3), and the general architectures used for this granularity level (Section 4.5) with popular feature sets (Section 4.4) and evaluation methods (Section 4.6). Finally, we present state-of-the-art results in Section 4.7.

4.2   APPLICATIONS

As previously mentioned, document-level QE has been less explored than word and sentence-level QE. Consequently, less work has been done and fewer applications explored for this level.

The most straightforward application for document-level QE is *gisting*. As motivation, Soricut and Echihabi [2010] have an e-service that hosts travelers' reviews about restaurants, hotels, etc. The majority of the reviews may be written in English, but there may be a large amount of users of this e-service that do not speak English and would need to have access to such reviews in their own native language. The vast number of reviews are simply too large for human translation, making this a perfect scenario for MT. The drawback is that the quality of the machine translation needs to be assessed somehow. The seller of a product or the service provider would not want to have the reputation of their product/service diminished because of low quality translations. Moreover, the quality of single sentences and/or words is less relevant in this scenario: For the end-user the main message is what is important. Therefore, a system able to score entire reviews according to their quality for the end-user is the ideal tool. Such a system could then be used to select only a handful of reviews for publication in a different language: those predicted as having good translation quality. In addition to user-generated reviews, other on-line services could benefit from document-level QE, such as blogs, market place platforms, and so on.

Another application suggested by Scarton [2017] is the use of document-level QE for estimating the effort of a full translation job. It is common practice in the MT industry to sub-contract freelancers to perform a post-editing task. It is also common for them to deal with sensitive or confidential information and, consequently, the post-editors receive sentences in rrandomized order for post-editing. The assumption is that when the sentences are put back in their document context, there will still be errors that could only be solved with document-wide information. Therefore, a reviewer (usually an internal translator) performs the task of further correcting the post-edited documents in order to make them publishable. An ideal QE system for this full process would need to deal not only with word- or sentence-level problems, but also with the remaining problems at document level. A two-stage post-editing method [Scarton et al., 2015b], presented in Section 4.3, can be used for this purpose since it encompasses information about the full post-editing and reviewing process.

4.3   LABELS

Labels for document-level QE need to take into account the quality of entire documents. As shown by Scarton et al. [2015b], asking humans for a single score for the entire document that encompasses its overall quality is not feasible. Humans may get confused or distracted by problems at other lower levels and, consequently, be misled in their assessment. Therefore, document-level evaluation (in general) is less trivial than the evaluation of more fine-grained levels.

Three types of labels have been explored for document-level QE: reference-based metrics, such as BLEU [Bojar et al., 2015, Scarton and Specia, 2014a, Soricut and Echihabi, 2010], marks from reading comprehension tests [Scarton and Specia, 2016], and a variation of HTER from a two-stage post-editing method [Scarton et al., 2015b].

Although BLEU-style metrics have been used in early work on this topic, they are not reliable as a measure of document quality. Such metrics are limited by the use of human references and only perform matches between MT output and such references. Therefore, they are usually agnostic to a specific task. For instance, what does a 0.6 BLEU score mean for the end-user? It says very little about the usefulness of the MT output for the end-user or even for post-editing. In addition, metrics like BLEU are also unable to capture differences among documents translated by the same (or very similar) MT system(s), which can be a problem for several applications. Scarton [2017] shows that label variation in datasets with different documents machine translated by a given MT system is very low when BLEU-style metrics are used to evaluate them.

Finally, one of the advantages of QE is that it enables task-based evaluation with relatively few annotated data points. Therefore, it is possible to use more informative labels that are suitable for a given task. These, however, tend to be more expensive to collect than automatic metrics. In what follows, we describe two types of labels.

4.3.1   LABELS FOR EVALUATING *GISTING*

For the evaluation of MT for *gisting* purposes at document level, previous work has used reading comprehension tests [Berka et al., 2011, Jones et al., 2005a,b]. The intuition behind this approach is that if a test taker can correctly answer questions about a document based solely on its machine-translated version in their native language, the quality of such a document is good for the purposes of *gisting*; otherwise, the quality of the output is considered bad. In order to avoid biases introduced by specific test takers, answers by multiple test takers on each given translated document can be collected and their marks averaged. In the context of QE, the idea is to take an aggregated score that represents the marks received by test takers for all questions in a questionnaire on a given document as a quality label. A dataset of multiple documents with labels collected in this fashion could then be used to train a QE model to predict such aggregated marks.

This type of evaluation is, however, time-consuming and expensive, as reading comprehension questions must first be devised, and questions need to be marked. The latter task is minimized if multiple-choice questions are used, but this type of question is limited in its capacity to capture text understanding, with guessing often playing a major role. In addition, it requires the creation of plausible distractors for each correct answer, which is also time consuming. Given that small datasets may be enough for document-level QE, previous work has used reading comprehension test marks as labels for document-level QE [Scarton, 2017, Scarton and Specia, 2016].

The type of label will depend on the type of question. If questions are open, labels are more likely to be real values, e.g., an average score of the marks for all questions. On the other hand, if multiple choice questions are used, more natural labels are a discrete value indicating the (normalized) count of correct answers. The type of question should also play an important role in the performance of the test takers, and therefore in how its contribution is accounted for in the final marks. Scarton [2017], following the work of Meurers et al. [2011] on the effect of different types of questions, proposes to incorporate the information about different types of questions into the document scores. The CREG-MT-eval dataset [Scarton and Specia, 2016], that is a version of the CREG corpus [Ott et al., 2012], is used for this work. CREG is a reading comprehension corpus for second-language learners of German created with the aim of building and evaluating systems that automatically correct answers to questions. Questions were manually created by experts in the area of second-language learner proficiency assessment for each document in this corpus. CREG has three types of questions: literal, reorganization, and inference (from simpler to more complex). CREG-MT-eval is a selection of 208 documents from CREG, machine translated by 4 different MT systems into English. The questions for each document were professionally translated. Test takers were recruited to answer reading comprehension questions based on the machine-translated documents. The questions were marked according to a scale that varied between 0 (incorrect) and 1 (perfect). Scarton [2017] learns weights for each type of question in CREG-MT-eval, using random search [Bergstra and

Bengio, 2012] and optimizing toward MAE or Pearson's r. Equation (4.1) shows the function proposed to devise a quality score for each document:

$$ f = \alpha \cdot \frac{1}{Nl} \sum_{k=1}^{Nl} lq_k + \beta \cdot \frac{1}{Nr} \sum_{k=1}^{Nr} rq_k + \gamma \cdot \frac{1}{Ni} \sum_{k=1}^{Ni} iq_k, \qquad (4.1) $$

where Nl, Nr, and Ni are the number of "literal", "reorganization", and "inference" questions, respectively, lq_k, rq_k, and iq_k are real values between 0 and 1, according to the mark of question k, and α, β, and γ are weights for the different types of questions.

To illustrate the creation of labels from reading comprehension tests, Table 4.2 (extracted from Scarton and Specia [2016]) shows an example of a document in German (SRC), its machine-translated (MT) and human-translated (REF) versions in English, as well as the manually translated questions. The human translation is only shown for reference. In the data collection process, it was used as control group. It is possible to observe that, based only on the MT output (plus potentially world knowledge), it is very difficult (or impossible) to answer questions 2, 3, and 4. Therefore, the quality scores based on the reading comprehension questions answered using the MT output will be lower than if the human translation (or a better machine translation) is used. We highlight the answers or clues for answers in the reference translation in Table 4.2. The answers are explicit in the text, however, the machine translated version does not contain the correct information. In this case, the problem is that the key sentences for answering questions 2, 3, and 4 were poorly translated, which is a typical case of MT for *gisting*: There is no need for all the sentences to be correctly translated, although it is important that the sentences including the desirable information are adequate. For instance, the quality of sentences 1, 5, and 6 is irrelevant for answering the questions. Therefore, reading comprehension evaluation seems to be a more reliable option to evaluate the quality of machine-translated documents with the purpose of *gisting* than labels that aggregate sentence-level scores.

4.3.2   LABELS FOR MEASURING POST-EDITING EFFORT

If the purpose of the evaluation is to estimate post-editing cost, or the total cost of a translation job—as mentioned in Section 4.2, a task-based method that relies on a post-editing workflow is needed. Scarton et al. [2015b] propose a two-stage post-editing method to deal with this challenge. In the first step of this method (PE1), sentences are post-edited in random order, without document context. In the second stage (PE2), the post-edited sentences are put back in their original order and then sent for post-editing again as a document. The motivation for this method was to understand the linguistic issues that can only be solved with access to the entire discourse, which would provide evidence on how a document-level score can be more than the aggregation of the scores of its sentences when accessed independently.

To illustrate the concept behind this method, Table 4.3 (extracted from Scarton et al. [2015b]) shows an example of changes from PE1 to PE2, both in German (DE), related to discourse phenomena along with the source (SRC), English (EN). The text in bold in this table

Table 4.2: Example of a document in the CREG corpus and its machine translation (extracted from Scarton and Specia [2016])

SRC (DE)	1- Objektbeschreibung einer 15-jährigenWohneinheit 2-Am Ende der Straße umgeben von Einfamilienhäusern erreichen Sie Ihr neues Heim. 3- Von der Eingangstür treten Sie in den oberen Bereich dieser wunderbarenWohneinheit , die die Eigentümer sehr sorgfältig und mit Liebe zum Detail removiert haben. 4- Im Erdgeschoss befinden sich ein Bad mit Tageslicht, Gäste WC, die Küche und ein äußerst geräumiges Wohn/Esszimmer mit faszinierendem Blick auf den gepflegten Garten. 5- Die Treppe hinunter sind ein weiteres Bad mit Dusche - bisher noch nicht benutzt - sowie zwei gleich große Räume, beide mit Blick auf den herrlichen Garten und das angrenzendeWaldgebiet. 6- Die Zimmer in diesem Bereich sind in hochwertigem Laminat ausgelegt. 7- Wenn Sie verkehrsgünstig wohnen möchten und gleichzeitig eine familiäre Umgebung schätzen, ist dieseWohnung für Sie richtig.
MT (EN)	1- Description a 15-year residential unit 2- At the end of the street surrounded by family houses you reach your new home. 3- From the front door you enter into the upper region of this wonderful residential unit who remo four very carefully and with attention to detail the owners. 4- Downstairs there is a bathroom with daylight, guest toilet, kitchen and an extremely spacious living/dining room with a fascinating view are the landscaped garden. 5- The stairs are a further bathroom with shower–not yet used–and two equally sized rooms, both overlooking the beautiful garden and the adjacent forest. 6- The rooms in this area are designed in high-quality laminate. 7- If you want to stay conveniently and simultaneously appreciate a family environment, this apartment is right for you.
REF (EN)	1- Property description for a 15-year-old residential unit 2- Your new home is at the end of the street surrounded by **(Q1) single-family homes**. 3-When you enter the front door, you find yourself on the upper floor of this wonderful property which the owners have carefully **(Q2) renovated** and decorated with much attention to detail. 4- The **(Q3) ground floor has a bathroom with natural light, a guest toilet, the kitchen and a spacious living/dining room** with a fascinating view of the beautiful garden. 5- Downstairs you will find an additional bathroom with shower (that has not yet been used) and two equally large bedrooms overlooking the wonderful garden. 6- The downstairs rooms have high-quality laminate flooring. 7- If you want to enjoy the benefits of a convenient location with a **(Q4) suburban flair,** this property is perfect for you.
Questions	1- For whom is this apartment ideal? 2- Is the apartment in a new building or an old building? 3- Name two rooms on the ground floor. 4-Where is the apartment?

Table 4.3: Example of changes from PE1 to PE2 (extracted from Scarton et al. [2015b])

PE1 (DE)	1- St. Petersburg bietet nicht viel kulturelles Angebot, Moskau hat viel mehr Kultur, es hat eine Grundlage.
	2- Es ist schwer für die Kunst, sich in unserem Umfeld durchzusetzen .
	3- Wir brauchen das kulturelle Fundament, aber wir haben jetzt mehr Schriftsteller als Leser.
	4- **Das ist falsch**.
	5- In Europa gibt es viele neugierige Menschen, die auf Kunstausstellungen , Konzerte gehen.
	6- **Hier ist diese Schicht ist dünn**.
PE2 (DE)	1- St. Petersburg bietet nicht viel kulturelles Angebot, Moskau hat viel mehr Kultur, es hat eine Grundlage.
	2- Es ist schwer für die Kunst, sich in unserem Umfeld durchzusetzen .
	3- Wir brauchen das kulturelle Fundament, aber wir haben jetzt mehr Schriftsteller als Leser.
	4- **Das ist nicht gut**.
	5- In Europa gibt es viele neugierige Menschen, die auf Kunstausstellungen , Konzerte gehen.
	6- **Hier ist die Anzahl solcherMenschen gering**.
SRC (EN)	1- St. Petersburg is not a cultural capital, Moscow has much more culture, there is bedrock there.
	2- It's hard for art to grow on our rocks.
	3- We need cultural bedrock, but we now have more writers than readers.
	4- **This is wrong**.
	5- In Europe, there are many curious people, who go to art exhibits, concerts.
	6- **Here, this layer is thin**.

shows the segments that were changed from PE1 to PE2. First, sentence (4) in PE1 is a literal translation of *"This is wrong"* and it was changed in PE2 (4) to better fit into the context, because it gives the sense of *"This is not good"*. Second, sentence (6) in PE1—literal translation of *"Here, this layer is thin"*—was corrected in PE2 (4) in order to better fit the context of the paragraph, having the meaning: *"Here, the number of such people is low"*. It is important to highlight that in both cases the changes could only be performed with document context. The sentences in PE1 are not incorrect translations in terms of grammar or word choice at sentence level, however, they do not fit in the context of the surrounding sentences.

One open issue in this two-stage post-editing approach is how to extract quality labels from this data. The solution proposed by Scarton [2017] and used at WMT16 [Bojar et al., 2016] is to compute HTER scores between the results of PE1 and the machine translation ($PE_1 \times MT$) and between PE1 and PE2 ($PE_2 \times PE_1$). Then, these two values are linearly combined and weights are learned for each component, as shown in Equation (4.2), where w_2 and w_1 are empirically defined:

$$f = w_1 \cdot PE_1 \times MT + w_2 \cdot PE_2 \times PE_1. \qquad (4.2)$$

4.4   FEATURES

Work on features for document-level QE follows, to a large degree, work on features for sentence-level QE. Although discourse-level features have been explored for document-level QE [Scarton, 2017], the majority of features for this level are based on shallow linguistic information.

As previously defined in Section 3.4, features for QE can be broadly divided into four categories: confidence features, fluency features, complexity features, and adequacy features, with the latter three types being explored for document-level QE, along with additional features that rely on external MT systems or word embedding representations. We also present separately features that attempt to capture discourse information.

4.4.1   COMPLEXITY FEATURES

Complexity features are extracted from the source document only to capture the difficulty of translating such a text. Some examples used for document-level QE are:

- number of tokens in the source document;

- average number of translations per source word in the source document using probabilistic dictionaries;

- average frequency of bigrams in the document that fall in the first quartile of frequency in a large corpus of the source language;

- average frequency of words in the source document using a large corpus of the source language;

- LM probability/perplexity of n-grams in the source document using a large corpus of the source language to build the LM;

- average likelihood of parse trees for sentences in the source document as given by a probabilistic parser; and

- number of pronouns.

4.4.2   FLUENCY FEATURES

Fluency features are extracted from the target sentence only and aim to capture the likelihood of the translation being a text found in the target language. Examples explored for document-level QE include:

- number of tokens in the target document;

- number of punctuation marks in the target document;

- number of content words in the target document;

- proportion of out-of-vocabulary tokens in the target document, i.e., tokens in the source language;

- number of sentences in the target document;

- LM probability/perplexity of n-grams in the target document using a large corpus of the target language to build the LM;

- LM probability/perplexity of n-grams of POS tags in the target document using a large corpus of POS-tagged target language to build the LM;

- average likelihood of parse trees for sentences in the target document as given by a probabilistic parser; and

- number of pronouns.

4.4.3   ADEQUACY FEATURES

Adequacy features combine information from the source and the target documents. They are usually based on differences or ratios of source and target language features. Examples of adequacy features used for document-level QE are:

- ratio between the number of tokens in the source document and the number of tokens in the target document;

- ratio of the number of content words in the source document and the number of content words in the target document;

- Kullback-Leibler divergence between a source document and a target document document topic distribution (topic distributions are extracted using latent Dirichlet allocation (LDA));

- Jensen-Shannon divergence between a source document and a target document document topic distribution (topic distributions are extracted using LDA);

- ratio of content word repetition between the target and source documents;

- ratio of content lemma repetition between the target and source documents; and

- ratio of noun repetition between the target and source documents.

4.4.4   DISCOURSE-AWARE FEATURES

Scarton and Specia [2014a] propose two sets of features to assess text cohesion. These features rely on POS information and can be used for measuring complexity, fluency, and adequacy. The first set of features consider word repetition. A document that presents high scores for repetition is expected to have high lexical cohesion. The word repetition features are as follows.

- **Average word repetition:** For each content word, its frequency within the document is counted. Then, the repetition counts are summed and divided by the total number of content words in the document. This feature can be computed for the source and target documents.

- **Average lemma repetition:** The same as word repetition, but the words are first lemmatized.

- **Average noun repetition:** The same as word repetition, but only nouns are considered.

- **Ratios:** The ratio values between source and target word, lemma, or noun repetitions.

The second set of features uses latent semantic analysis (LSA) [Landauer and Dumais, 1997] for assessing document cohesion. LSA aims to capture the topic of texts based on the words that these texts contain. This method is based on singular vector decomposition (SVD) for dimensionality reduction. It is a robust method where texts can be full documents, paragraphs, or sentences. An LSA matrix can be built considering $words \times sentences$, $words \times paragraphs$, $words \times documents$, etc. In the case of $words \times sentence$, each cell contains the frequency of a given word in a given sentence. LSA was originally designed to be used with large corpora of multiple documents (topic modeling). In Scarton and Specia [2014a], however, since the aim is to measure coherence within documents, an LSA $words \times sentences$ matrix is computed for each individual document. Scarton [2017] also worked with these features and made some extensions. The LSA features are as follows.

- **LSA cohesion—adjacent sentences (Spearman's ρ):** For each sentence in a document, the Spearman's ρ rank correlation coefficient is calculated between its word vector and the word vectors of its adjacent neighbors (sentences which appear immediately before and after the given sentence). For sentences with two neighbors (most cases), the correlation values are averaged. After that, the values for all sentences in the document are averaged in order to have a single figure for the entire document.

- **LSA cohesion—adjacent sentences (cosine distance):** The same as above, but the cosine distance is applied instead of Spearman's ρ rank correlation.

- **LSA cohesion—all sentences (Spearman's ρ):** For each sentence in a document, the Spearman's ρ rank correlation coefficient is calculated between the word vectors of a given sentence and the word vectors of all the others. The values for all sentences in the document are then averaged.

- **LSA cohesion—all sentences (cosine distance):** The same as above, the cosine distance is applied instead of Spearman's ρ rank correlation.

Scarton [2017] introduces a set of discourse-aware source features based on syntactic parser and Rhetorical Structure Theory (RST) parser information. In theory, such features can be applied to both source and target documents, as shown in Scarton and Specia [2015]. However, due to the performance of the parsers on the—at the time—numerous problematic machine translated sentences in the target language, these features proved more effective for source documents. These can be seen, therefore, as a special type of complexity feature. In addition, these features are highly language dependent since they require robust parsers to be extracted. The list of discourse-aware features for the source document in English includes the following.

- Number of *expansion* connectives: discourse relations where a second argument expands the first argument (e.g., *in addition*).[1]

- Number of *contingency* connectives: discourse relations where one of the situations described in an argument causes or influence another argument (e.g., *because*).

- Number of *comparison* connectives: discourse relations where two arguments are compared (e.g., *although*).

- Number of *temporal* connectives: discourse relations where the arguments are related temporally (e.g., *when*).

- Number of connectives: sum of the values for all the above types of connectives.

- Number of *non-discourse* connectives: some discourse connectives are ambiguous and my assume roles other than connectives, for example, *once* can be a temporal connective or an adverb meaning *formerly* [Pitler and Nenkova, 2009].

- Number of elementary discourse unit (EDU) breaks: EDUs are the minimum units of text that assume some discourse role. In the following example, there are three EDU breaks: *"However , **EDU_BREAK** despite the economic success, **EDU_BREAK** it has become increasingly clear **EDU_BREAK** that Blair was over ."*

---

[1]Connective-related features can be extracted using either pre-defined lists (e.g., the lists used in the Coh-metrix tool: http://141.225.41.245/cohmetrixhome/documentation_indices.html) or parsers (e.g., Pitler and Nenkova's parser: http://www.cis.upenn.edu/~nlp/software/discourse.html).

- Number of *nucleus* relations in the RST tree for the entire document. Figure 4.1 shows an example of an RST relation between two EDUs, where *"Brown has coveted the office of Prime Minister since May 12, 1994, the fateful day"* is the *nucleus* of the RST relation.

- Number of *satellite* relations in the RST tree for the entire document. Figure 4.1 shows an example of an RST relation between two EDUs, where *"when John Smith, the Lor leader in opposition, died of a heart attack."* is the *satellite* of the RST relation.

- Height of the RST tree.

- Number of subtrees in the RST tree.

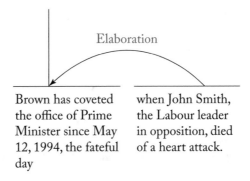

Figure 4.1: Example of RST relation between two EDUs.

4.4.5   WORD EMBEDDING FEATURES

Word embeddings can also be used as features for document-level QE. Scarton et al. [2016] propose the use of averaged word embeddings at document level. In this approach, word vectors are extracted following standard word embedding tools. For example, Scarton et al. [2016] use *word2vec* [Mikolov et al., 2013b] with the continuous bag-of-words model. This involves averaging all of the word vectors in the document, generating a single vector for the document. Such averaged word vectors can be extracted for both source and target documents and, therefore, they can be used to measure fluency, complexity, or even adequacy by measuring the distance between source and target word vectors. For document-level QE, word embeddings were used as complexity and fluency features [Scarton, 2017, Scarton et al., 2016].

4.4.6   CONSENSUS AND PSEUDO-REFERENCE FEATURES

As previously mentioned, pseudo-reference features have been used extensively for sentence- and word-level QE. Pseudo-references were first used in the context of QE for document-level QE in Soricut and Echihabi [2010]. In addition to proposing such features, Soricut and Echihabi

[2010] emphasize the importance of the pseudo-references being generated by MT system(s) which are as different as possible from the MT system of interest, and preferably of much better quality. This should ensure that string similarity features (like BLEU) indicate more than simple consensus between two similar MT systems, which would produce the same (possibly bad quality) translations.

Scarton [2017] proposes the use of consensus among different MT systems: If various different MT systems output the same target, the respective target may be correct. In this case, the quality of the various off-the-shelf systems does not need to be given.

BLEU, TER, and Meteor (Metric for Evaluation of Translation with Explicit ORdering) [Denkowski and Lavie, 2011] are the automatic metrics previously used as pseudo-reference-based features for document-level QE [Scarton, 2017, Scarton and Specia, 2014a, Soricut and Echihabi, 2010]. However, any automatic metric may be used for the same purpose, e.g., Scarton and Specia [2014b] use metrics based on syntactic similarities from shallow and dependency parser information.

4.5   ARCHITECTURES

Similarly to sentence-level QE, architectures for document-level QE are directly related to the type of quality label being predicted. For instance, if the label follows a continuous distribution or an ordered scale, the most widely used method is regression. On the other hand, if the label is categorical (non-ordinal), the method applied is classification.

For treating the task as a regression problem, in principle any regression algorithm can be applied. Previous work used M5P regression trees [Soricut and Echihabi, 2010], Bayesian ridge regression [Scarton et al., 2015a], extremely rrandomized trees [Biçici, 2016], SVM [Biçici, 2016, Biçici et al., 2015, Scarton, 2017, Scarton et al., 2016, Scarton and Specia, 2014a, Scarton et al., 2015a], and GPs [Scarton, 2017, Scarton et al., 2016] methods, with the latter two dominating most approaches.

Feature selection techniques were also explored for document-level QE, including: recursive feature elimination [Biçici, 2016, Biçici et al., 2015], dimensionality reduction with partial least squares [Biçici, 2016, Biçici et al., 2015], backward feature selection [Scarton et al., 2015a], and exhaustive search [Scarton et al., 2015a]. Previous work that used GPs also explored feature combination considering different kernels for different feature types, i.e., handcrafted features were handled by one kernel, while word-embedding features or pseudo-reference-based features were modeled in another kernel [Scarton, 2017, Scarton et al., 2016].

For classification, while any algorithm is applicable in principle, existing work explores random forests, SVMs and ordinal classification [Scarton, 2017]. Both random forests and SVMs treat the problem as a multi-class classification task in which the classes do not follow any order, while the ordinal logistic model is able to take the order of the classes into account. Since the labels have an order, ordinal classification is expected to be the most suitable approach.

One potentially promising approach is to use fine-grained prediction levels in order to improve document-level QE. For instance, a sequential prediction of paragraphs, sentences or words could be used in the architecture to enhance prediction at document level. A starting point in this direction could be the work on joint word- and sentence-level prediction by Kim et al. [2017b], but it is not clear whether this would generalize for documents. In addition, the approach would require data annotated at document level and at the finer-grained levels, which is not yet available.

4.6 EVALUATION

The evaluation of document-level QE is also dependent on the type of label predicted and the ML approach used. When using regression approaches for predicting continuous labels, document-level QE is evaluated in the same way presented in Section 3.6 for both scoring and ranking tasks.

As in sentence-level QE, document-level QE has adopted the Pearson's r correlation coefficient as the primary metric and MAE and RMSE are complementary metrics. For evaluating rankings of documents, Spearman's ρ rank correlation coefficient is used as the primary metric with DeltaAvg as secondary metric.

When the quality label considered is categorical and classification is applied, precision, recall, and F-measure are used to evaluate the performance of the QE models, as in the work of Scarton [2017].

4.7 STATE-OF-THE-ART RESULTS

In what follows we describe the best systems in the two editions of the WMT shared tasks that included either paragraph- or document-level QE. In addition, we include the work of Scarton [2017] on document-level QE, which represents the best systems for predicting variants of post-editing effort and reading comprehension scores.

4.7.1 REFERENTIAL TRANSLATION MACHINES

The WMT15 shared task focused on paragraph-level QE. The paragraphs were extracted from the WMT13 news translation corpus. Taking the machine translations from all participating systems, for each source language paragraph, a machine-translated version was randomly chosen from the set of systems. Given a paragraph, participants were required to predict its Meteor score, which was computed based on the WMT13 news reference corpus. Two language pairs were included: English-German and German-English with 1,215 sentences per language pair. Paragraphs were composed of 1–16 sentences. MAE was used as the official evaluation metric.

The winning system applies referential translation machines (RTMs) [Biçici et al., 2015]. RTMs [Biçici, 2013, Biçici and Way, 2014] aim to identify "acts of translation" when translating from a given language into another using an external corpus (in the same domain) as reference.

External data is used to select "interpretants" that contain data close to both training and test sets to provide context for similarity comparison. In other words, interpretants are data instances close to both training and test sets under investigation. These interpretants can then be used as (pseudo) references for similarity calculation and for providing context [Biçici, 2013].

The steps, according to Biçici [2015], are as follows.

1. ParFDA(*train*, *test*, $\mathcal{C}$) $\rightarrow \mathcal{I}$.

2. MTPP($\mathcal{I}$, *train*) $\rightarrow \mathcal{F}_{train}$.

3. MTPP($\mathcal{I}$, *test*) $\rightarrow \mathcal{F}_{test}$.

4. learn(M, $\mathcal{F}_{train}$) $\rightarrow \mathcal{M}$.

5. predict($\mathcal{M}$, $\mathcal{F}_{test}$) $\rightarrow \hat{q}$.

First, interpretants ($\mathcal{I}$) that are relevant to both training and test sets are selected. This is achieved using a corpus ($\mathcal{C}$, in the same domain as training and test dataset) and the parallel Feature Decay Algorithm (FDA) [Biçici et al., 2014]. FDA is an approach for instance selection that aims to increase the diversity of data. Then, in steps 2 and 3, a MTPP (Machine Translation Performance Predictor) uses $\mathcal{I}$ to extract features for both training and test sets ($\mathcal{F}_{train}$ and $\mathcal{F}_{test}$, respectively). Such features will be in a space where similarities between acts can be extracted. In step 4, $\mathcal{F}_{train}$ is used as input for a learning algorithm (M), in order to build a prediction model ($\mathcal{M}$). Finally, $\mathcal{M}$ is used to predict the quality ($\hat{q}$) of $\mathcal{F}_{test}$.

Features for source and target paragraphs capture coverage, LM perplexity, translation probability, similarity between vector representations and sentence length, among others. Feature selection is performed using a recursive feature elimination method. The winning ML models for both language pairs use SVM.

RTMs have been used in several WMT QE shared tasks for predicting the quality of all granularity levels. It is robust since the MTPP module can encompass different types of features. However, the need of in-domain external data is a drawback. The need for features to be in the same space for similarity calculation also adds to its complexity.

4.7.2 DOCUMENT EMBEDDINGS

The WMT16 shared task on document-level QE addressed prediction for full documents. The data consisted of entire documents evaluated using the two-stage post-editing method [Scarton, 2017, Scarton et al., 2015b] introduced in Section 4.3. The language pair was English-Spanish, with a set of 208 post-edited documents. These documents were extracted from the English-Spanish WMT news translation task data between 2008 and 2013. Given all system submissions for all documents in all the years of the news task, a translation generated by a random MT system was selected for each source document. The w_1 and w_2 parameters of Equation (4.2) were derived empirically: w_1 was fixed to 1, while w_2 was optimized in order to meet two criteria.

First, the final label should lead to significant data variation in terms of standard deviation from the mean document-level score. Second, the difference between the MAE of a mean baseline and the MAE of the official baseline QE system should be sufficiently large.[2] The mean baseline is built by using the mean value of the training set labels as the predicted value to all instances of the test set. The official baseline QE system was built with 17 commonly used features that are adaptations of sentence-level features, so-called baseline features:

- number of tokens in the target document;

- number of tokens in the source document;

- average source token length;

- type/token ratio (number of occurrences of the target word within the target hypothesis, averaged for all words in the hypothesis);

- LM probability of target document;

- LM probability of source document;

- average number of translations per source word in the document;

- average number of translations per source word in the document weighted by the inverse frequency of each word in the source corpus;

- percentage of unigrams/bigrams/trigrams in quartile 1 of frequency in a corpus of the source language;

- percentage of unigrams/bigrams/trigrams in quartile 4 of frequency in a corpus of the source language;

- percentage of unigrams in the source document seen in a corpus of the source language;

- number of punctuation marks in target document; and

- number of punctuation marks in source document.

Two systems achieved the best results in the competition. Scarton et al. [2016] combine these 17 baseline features with word embeddings from the English source documents and build a model using GP as the algorithm. The word embeddings were learned by using the CBOW model trained on a very large corpus. Document embeddings were extracted by averaging the word embeddings of the document. The GP model was trained with two kernels: one for the 17 baseline features and another for the 500 features from word embeddings. Since each kernel has its own set of hyperparameters, the full model leverages the contributions from the two different feature sets.

[2] $w_2 = 13$ was the best result.

The other winning system [Biçici, 2016] uses RTMs as previously presented in Section 4.7.1. For this submission, after feature selection, a dimensionality reduction and mapping step using partial least square (PLS) is applied. PLS is a technique for feature selection that maps the source features into a latent space by also using information from target features. An interactive process of orthogonalisation followed by vector selection are used to generate the latent features [Biçici et al., 2013]. Extremely rrandomized trees, an ensemble method similar to random forests, is used for building the prediction model.

The Scarton et al. [2016] system is simple and does not require complex ML approaches nor complex feature engineering. However, as is the case for solutions using word embeddings, it is not easily interpretable. For instance, it is hard to define why averaged word embeddings work for this context, and the only way to select the parameters for training the embeddings is empirically. The advantages and disadvantages of RTMs were discussed in Section 4.7.1.

4.7.3 BEST POST-EDITING EFFORT AND *GISTING* SYSTEMS

Scarton [2017] presents a benchmark performance of different systems with several variations of the label derived from Equation (4.2), repeated below for ease of reference. The best system in the WMT16 dataset outperforms the two winning systems of the shared task. It is built with all document-level features from the publicly available QuEst++ toolkit (Section 6.2) using GP as the algorithm.

$$f = w_1 \cdot PE_1 \times MT + w_2 \cdot PE_2 \times PE_1. \tag{4.3}$$

In addition, two quality labels devised from Equation (4.3) for the same dataset used in the WMT16 shared task are proposed.

- **DISS-LC-P:** w_1 varies from 0.0 to 1.0 ($w_2 = 1 - w_1$), and f is chosen in order to maximize Pearson's r for a baseline QE model built with the 17 baseline features listed previously using SVM. 10-fold cross-validation was applied in the data and Pearson's r are averages of all folds.

- **DISS-LC-M:** w_1 was also rrandomized between 0.0 and 1.0 but instead of maximizing Pearson's r, the difference between the MAE of a mean baseline and the MAE of the baseline QE model was maximized. The mean baseline is built by using the mean value of the training set labels as the predicted value for all instances of the test set.

For both labels, the best models use GPs with one kernel for all QuEst++ features and another kernel for discourse-aware features (presented in Section 4.4.4).

Focusing on reading comprehension tests, Scarton [2017] builds models for two types of corpus: CREG and MCtest [Richardson et al., 2013]. For CREG, since the questions allow open answers, Equation (4.1) was used to devise the quality labels.

- **RC-CREG-P:** Random search [Bergstra and Bengio, 2012] is used to maximize the Pearson's r correlation coefficient between a baseline QE model built with the 17 baseline features and the true labels. At each iteration, α is chosen randomly from the range [0.0, 1.0).

Another value ϕ was chosen randomly (also from the range [0.0, 1.0)) in order to define β as $(1 - \alpha) \cdot \phi$ and γ as $(1 - \alpha) \cdot (1 - \phi)$. A baseline QE model built with the 17 baseline features and SVM was trained at each iteration with 10-fold cross-validation applied and the Pearson's r correlation coefficients were the average of all folds.

- **RC-CREG-M:** Random search is used to maximize the difference between the MAE of a mean baseline and the MAE of the baseline QE model. The mean baseline is built by using the mean value of the training set labels as the predicted value to all instances of the test set. The parameters are derived similarly to RC-CREG-P and a similar QE model is built at each iteration.

The best model for RC-CREG-P was built with SVM and the 17 baseline features combined with document embeddings from the source and from the target documents. For RC-CREG-M, the best model was built with GP and all document-level features available in QuEst++.

The MCtest corpus is composed of multiple choice questions. The quality labels derived for this dataset follow a discrete distribution, i.e., the number of correct answers. Each document has four questions, therefore the number of correct answers varies between 0 and 4. Scarton [2017] considers two cases: 5-class problem (each possible number of correct answers becomes a class) and 3-class problem (classes 0, 1, and 2 are grouped into a single class for low scoring results). The best system in the 5-class problem was built by combining the 17 baseline features with word embeddings at document level from both source and target documents. The classification algorithm used was random forests. For the three-class problem the best system was built with all features available in QuEst++ plus advanced linguistic features (pronouns, connectives and EDUs counts, and RST tree information). The classification algorithm was also random forests.

The QE systems proposed by Scarton [2017] are straightforward and simple to reproduce. The main drawback is that the discourse-aware features require advanced NLP resources to be computed. This limits the approach to languages for which resources are available.

CHAPTER 5

Quality Estimation for other Applications

In this chapter we describe QE work for language output applications other than MT, namely Text Simplification (TS), Automatic Text Summarization (ATS), Grammatical Error Correction (GEC), Natural Language Generation (NLG), and Automatic Speech Recognition (ASR). Most of this work is very recent, with many opportunities for further development. Various approaches have been proposed for TS in the context of a shared task in 2016, while very little work could be found for the other areas. We hope that by providing this overview we will encourage researchers in these and other NLP applications to consider pursuing QE as an evaluation framework.

Our focus in this book is on texts produced by automatic applications, rather than by humans. A large body of work exists that targets grammatical error detection (often in conjunction with correction) as well as essay scoring in learner texts, i.e., texts written by those learning a second language.

Grammatical error detection focuses on spotting (and often fixing) grammar errors at the word or phrase level, in a similar fashion to subsentence-level QE but using fine-grained error categories rather than "good"/"bad" labels. Examples of error tag sets include five salient errors—determiner, preposition, noun number, verb form, and subject-verb agreement [Ng et al., 2013], and supersets of these with up to 80 categories of errors (pronouns, word choice, sentence structure, punctuation, capitalization, contractions, etc.) [Ng et al., 2014]. Recent work also includes a more holistic view of the problem than that of sentence-level grammaticality prediction. Methods that represent overall grammaticality include, for example, a 1–4-point scale score [Heilman et al., 2014] and the use of HTER on manually corrected sentences [Sakaguchi et al., 2016]. This resembles sentence-level MT QE work. Broadly speaking, many of these types of grammatical errors are also made by automatic applications. However, we believe that errors in human texts are much more subtle than those made by machines, and therefore different approaches are required. Additionally, detection is often just a component in systems where the final goal is to provide corrections that can then be used as feedback for learners. The QE for GEC systems that we introduce in Section 5.3 is different in the sense that it focuses on predicting the quality of texts generated by automatic systems that perform error correction, rather than the quality of the text originally written by learners.

Essay scoring consists in predicting a single score for an entire text (in literature, often a 5-paragraph essay), in a similar fashion to document-level QE for MT or ATS. Most work is done in the context of grading non-native speakers texts in standard language certificate tests [Burstein et al., 2013]. Different approaches range from heuristic methods that attempt to count different types of errors, including grammar, organization, usage, mechanics (e.g., capitalization), and style [Burstein et al., 2006] to ML methods that use a number of explicit features such as text length, coherence, cohesion, style, syntax, readability, n-grams, argumentation, etc. [Ghosh et al., 2016, Zesch et al., 2015] as well as learned features in neural models [Dong and Zhang, 2016, Taghipour and Ng, 2016]. The main difference between this line of work and that of QE at document level for tasks like MT is that the types of errors that are targeted by in essay scoring require deeper discourse processing and are often not present in the output of automatic systems. Essay scoring requires automatically representing deeper quality dimensions such as stance, organization, thesis clarity, argument persuasiveness, etc. [Persing and Ng, 2013, 2014, 2016a,b]. These dimensions are more applicable to the process of idea conceptualization when writing a text, and in particular, when writing with an essay on a specific topic, which makes essay scoring a very different task.

5.1 TEXT SIMPLIFICATION

Text Simplification is the task of applying transformations to a portion of text in order to make it more easily understandable by a certain target audience. Existing work can be classified into three categories.

- **Lexical simplification:** Consists in applying transformations to the words in a text, mainly by replacing complex words with simpler alternatives [Glavaš and Štajner, 2015, Horn et al., 2014, Paetzold and Specia, 2017]. By doing so, it is possible to adapt the vocabulary used in a text to suit the needs of a particular group of users, for example, children. This is done via heuristic and ML-based methods to find (or generate) and rank substitution candidates.

- **Syntactic simplification:** Consists in applying transformations that modify the syntactic structure of a text, normally a sentence [Angrosh et al., 2014, Siddharthan and Mandya, 2014]. Examples of the most common syntactic operations are sentence splitting, passive-to-active voice transformation, appositive clause removal, and pronoun resolution. This is normally done through explicit rules that can be either manually crafted or learned from data using grammar induction techniques.

- **Translation-based simplification:** An alternative to learning specific types of simplification transformations is to use a more general approach that will learn how to "translate" from complex to simple texts using complex-to-simple parallel corpora [Nisioi et al., 2017, Wubben et al., 2012, Xu et al., 2016]. The "translations" cover both the lexical and syntactic levels, in similar ways to MT approaches, except that both input and output texts are in the same language.

Figure 5.1 illustrates a sentence in the English language simplified in various ways. Much like MT systems, TS systems are also language output applications: They take as input an original sentence and produce as output a simpler version. Since TS approaches operate at the sentence level, QE systems can be very intuitively built for them.

In the sections that follow we consider all existing work in TS QE and describe the main applications (Section 5.1.1), labels (Section 5.1.2), features (Section 5.1.3), architectures (Section 5.1.4), and evaluation methods (Section 5.1.5) used in TS QE, and discuss the most effective approaches to this task (Section 5.1.6).

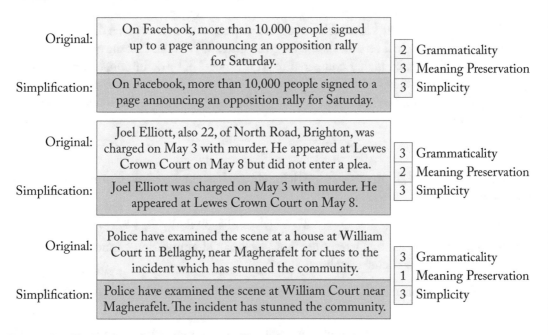

Figure 5.1: Examples of simplification in English.

5.1.1   APPLICATIONS

The potential applications of QE for TS are similar to the applications of MT QE. Quality estimates can be used by those interested in producing simplified versions of texts, including companies such as Newsela[1] and Guten,[2] which manually create adapted versions of news articles for readers with different reading levels. Although there is no evidence that these companies

[1] https://newsela.com
[2] https://gutennews.com.br

have been using automatic TS to increase simplification productivity, there is no reason why word-, phrase-, sentence-, or even document-level QE technologies could not be used in this way. QE technologies could also help improve the performance of different types of automatic TS systems. Take, for example, lexical simplification systems that replace single words with simpler alternatives. An effective word-level QE approach would be able to indicate whether or not the simplifier has made a mistake, which would consequently allow it to choose another replacement.

MT-based TS systems are able to produce multiple simplifications in the form of an n-best simplification list, hence a reliable sentence-level QE approach could help rerank them, potentially increasing the quality of the final output produced. Word- and phrase-level QE approaches could also help these and other types of TS systems by aiding in the decoding process.

Finally, QE for TS could be used to make a decision on whether a simplification, i.e., the simplified version of the text,[3] is reliable enough to be published as is or given directly to an end user, or whether the original version should be given instead. We note that the quality threshold for TS is likely to be much higher compared to MT. Since TS, by definition, assumes that the original text may be difficult to process by certain readers, a TS system that makes a mistake while simplifying such a text will make it even harder than its original version and, therefore, worse for the reader.

5.1.2   LABELS

The labels used by TS QE approaches are defined based on the three main properties deemed desirable for a high-quality simplified text.

- **Grammaticality:** Determines how grammatical the simplified text is.

- **Meaning preservation:** Determines how well the simplification captures the original meaning of the text being simplified.

- **Simplicity:** Determines how much easier simplification is in comparison to the original text.

These properties have been applied to collect manual annotations on the output of TS systems [Glavaš and Štajner, 2015, Paetzold and Specia, 2013]. Each automatically simplified sentence is judged with respect to each of these properties using a *Likert* scale, for example from 1–3 or 1–5. This type of evaluation has become standard in TS.

Using this type of manual evaluation, Štajner et al. [2014] devised the first sentence-level QE dataset for TS. Simplifications of 280 complex sentences were produced using various automatic simplification methods and then scored by humans on a 1–3-point scale with respect to grammaticality, meaning preservation, and simplicity. The scores for these properties can be interpreted as follows.

---

[3]We use the terms "simplification" and "simplified text/version" interchangeably, in the same way in which "machine translation" is used in the sense of a "machine-translated text".

- **Grammaticality:**

    1. ungrammatical,

    2. minor problems with grammaticality,

    3. grammatical.

- **Meaning preservation:**

    1. meaning is seriously changed or most of the relevant information lost,

    2. some of the relevant information is lost but the meaning of the remaining information is unchanged,

    3. all relevant information is kept without any change in meaning.

- **Simplicity:**

    1. a lot of irrelevant information is retained,

    2. some of irrelevant information is retained,

    3. all irrelevant information is eliminated.

This definition of simplicity focuses on how much irrelevant information the TS systems are able to discard. This notion of simplicity is closely connected to that of text compression and only applies to certain groups of readers, such as those who have issues with processing very long sentences. Other aspects should also be considered, such as the familiarity of words in a simplification, the complexity of its syntactic and semantic constructs, etc. Figure 5.2 shows a few annotations extracted from this dataset [Štajner et al., 2014].

Using these scores, two more label sets are inferred: Total3 and Total2. These label sets combine simplification properties in a single value. Total3 has three possible values.

- **OK:** Simplifications annotated with scores of value 3 for grammaticality and meaning preservation.

- **PE:** Simplifications that do not fulfill the requirements of the "OK" label, but that have a value of 2 or 3 for meaning preservation.

- **Dis:** Any other simplifications, i.e., the simplifications that have a value of 1 for meaning preservation.

These values were determined through an analysis of the dataset. The first two simplification examples in Figure 5.2 would be classified as "PE", since neither of them have a score of 3 for grammaticality and meaning preservation, and both have a 2 or 3 score for meaning preservation. The Total2 set was created with the goal of making the task of sentence-level QE for TS as simple as possible. Total2 has only two labels, which are inferred from the following Total3 labels.

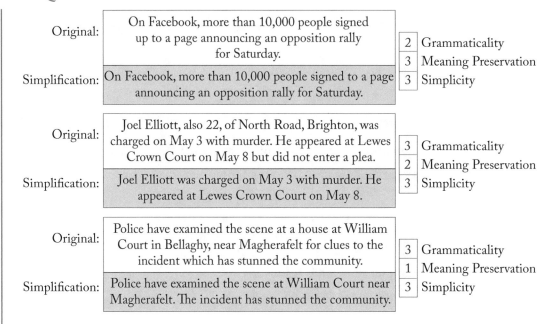

Figure 5.2: Instances from the QE dataset for TS in Štajner et al. [2014].

- **0:** Simplifications that received a "Dis" label in the Total3 set.

- **1:** Simplifications that received either a "PE" or "OK" label in the Total3 set.

Neither of these label sets incorporates simplicity. According to Štajner et al. [2014], these labels focus more on capturing whether or not the simplifications should be post-edited, hence they were created under the assumption that simplicity does not play a substantial role in this decision. Notice, however, that this is not necessarily true. Because the main purpose of simplifying a sentence is presenting its information in more accessible fashion, it is not reasonable to assume that a simplification that fails to do so is of good quality.

To address this issue, Štajner et al. [2016] collected a new dataset by combining three datasets introduced in previous work [Glavaš and Štajner, 2013, 2015, Štajner et al., 2015]. The instances in these datasets are composed of original sentences, simplified versions produced by a certain type of simplification approach, and *Likert* quality labels produced by human annotators for grammaticality, meaning preservation, and simplicity, using again 1–3 *Likert* scores.

Total3 and Total2 label sets were once again inferred from the original labels, but now incorporating simplicity. Total3 labels are defined as follows.

- **3:** Simplifications annotated with scores of 3 for grammaticality, meaning preservation and simplicity.

- **1:** Simplifications annotated with a score of 1 for either meaning preservation or simplicity.

- **2:** any other simplifications.

If the simplification is perfect in every aspect, it receives label 3. If it has either poor meaning preservation or simplicity, it receives label 1. The remaining simplifications receive label 2. Total2 labels are defined as follows.

- **0:** simplifications with a Total3 score of 1.

- **1:** remaining simplifications.

Using this dataset, Štajner et al. [2016] conduct the first shared task on sentence-level QE for TS, which was held at the 2016 workshop on Quality Assessment for Text Simplification (QATS 2016). The interpretation of the original 1–3 *Likert* labels for grammaticality, meaning preservation and simplification was said to be: 3 → "good", 2 → "ok", 1 → "bad". A fourth label that describes the overall quality of the simplification was also introduced. To that end, the 3/2/1 Total3 labels were mapped into "good"/"ok"/"bad" labels using the same transformation.

It is important to note that these labels do not take into account any particular use of the simplifications. Consider, for example, the sentence *"Her mother wanted her to leave school and marry, but she **rebelled**"* and its simplification *"Her mother wanted her to leave school and marry, but she **forced**"*, which were present in the dataset of Štajner et al. [2016]. This simplification received a "bad" label for simplicity and overall quality, which suggests that it would be better to discard it and simplify the original sentence from scratch. However, post-editing this simplification would not necessarily be difficult. This could be done by simply replacing *forced* with something simpler than *rebelled*, since the rest of the sentence would arguably not be challenging to most readers.

5.1.3 FEATURES

Sentence-level QE approaches for TS, much like from those for MT, need to use as input features that capture different aspects of the simplification being evaluated. As discussed in the previous section, the quality of an automatically produced simplification is commonly defined in terms of its grammaticality, meaning preservation, and simplicity. Features should thus attempt to capture these three quality dimensions to some extent.

Many of the features used for TS are similar to those used in MT QE. However, there are also many other interesting features that are unique to TS QE.

MT-Inspired Features
Most systems that participated in the sentence-level TS QE shared task held at QATS 2016 use at least a handful of features that are either commonly employed for MT or inspired by them, for example, length-based features:

- number of chunks, tokens, characters, word types, and punctuation markers in the original sentence;

- number of chunks, tokens, characters, word types, and punctuation markers in the simplified sentence;

- ratio between the number of chunks, tokens, characters, word types, and punctuation markers between the original and simplified sentences;

- average number of characters and syllables of the words in the original sentence;

- average number of characters and syllables of the words in the simplified sentence; and

- ratio between the average number of characters and syllables of the words in the original and simplified sentences.

Length-based features can help a QE model identify simplifications that are likely to be of poor quality. If the ratio between the number of tokens in the original and the simplified sentence is too far from one, the model might have cut off too many words from the original sentence. On the other hand, if the ratio is too close to one, it might be the case that the model was too conservative and did not perform enough simplification transformations.

Frequency-based and language model features are also popular:

- language model probability of the original sentence;

- language model probability of the simplified sentence;

- ratio between the language model probability of the original and simplified sentences;

- average language model probability of the words in the original sentence;

- average language model probability of the words in the simplified sentence;

- ratio between the average language model probability of the words in the original and simplified sentences;

- number of out-of-vocabulary words in the original sentence based on a language model of complex texts;

- number of out-of-vocabulary words in the simplification based on a language model of simplified texts; and

- percentage of words, bigrams, and trigrams in the simplified sentence with exceptionally high or low frequency a corpus of simplified texts.

The language model probability of a simplified sentence can offer very valuable information with respect to its grammaticality.

Based on parallel corpora containing complex sentences with simplified equivalents, such as the Wikipedia/Simple Wikipedia corpus [Kauchak, 2013] and the Newsela corpus [Newsela, 2016], translation probability tables can be generated. They allow the extraction of features such as:

- average translation probability between the words in the simplified sentence and the words aligned to them in the original sentence; and

- average number of translations of the words in the original sentence with a probability larger than α.

These features can be good indicators of meaning preservation. If the average translation probability is low, for example, it could mean that the simplification model failed to properly disambiguate the original sentence. Similarly, if the number of translations of the words in the source sentence is very high, then simplifying it could be hard, which increases the likelihood that the simplification model will make a mistake.

Another interesting set of MT-inspired features use MT evaluation metrics such as BLEU between the original and simplified sentences. Given that the original sentence and its simplification are written in the same language, such string similarity metrics can be used. BLEU for example is used to calculate the precision of n-grams in the system output with respect to those present in the original sentence. The resulting score is then used as a feature. A high BLEU score could indicate that the simplification is grammatical, since the system preserved the structure of the original sentence. A BLEU score that is too high, however, could mean that the system did not apply any transformations to the original sentence. In addition to BLEU, other metrics such as Meteor and TER have been used as features in TS QE.

We refer the reader to Popović and Štajner [2016] for an investigation on the correlation between these and many other MT evaluation metrics and TS QE scores for grammaticality, meaning preservation and simplicity. Štajner et al. [2014] and Popović and Štajner [2016] find that these metrics are best at capturing meaning preservation.

Semantic Features

A number of features have also be devised specifically for TS QE. Many of these features attempt to capture the semantic similarity between original and simplified sentences. The most frequently used semantic similarity features in TS QE are:

- TF-IDF cosine similarity between the original and simplified sentences using bag-of-words vectors with the words in these sentences, and alternatively with their synonyms;

- total, average, minimum, and maximum cosine similarity between the embeddings of all words in the original and simplified sentences; and

- total, average, minimum, and maximum cosine similarity between the embeddings of words in the original sentence that are aligned to words in the simplified sentence.

Instead of attempting to calculate similarity metrics between the original and the simplification, the semantic representations extracted to calculate these metrics can also be used in their raw form. Some frequent examples are:

- TF-IDF bag-of-words vectors representing the original sentence;

- TF-IDF bag-of-words vectors representing the simplified sentence;

- average embedding values of all words in the original sentence; and

- average embedding values of all words in the simplified sentence.

Syntactic Features

The syntactic structure of the original sentence and its simplified version also contains a number of clues that could help a QE system. Graesser et al. [2004] successfully exploit syntactic patterns extracted from constituency and dependency parses to quantify the cohesion and coherence of a sentence, two properties that could be seen as clues for grammaticality and meaning preservation.

Mathias and Bhattacharyya [2016] and Nisioi and Nauze [2016] introduce sentence-level QE approaches for TS that assess the constituency parses of the simplified sentences in order to estimate their structural complexity. The main features extracted from these parse trees are:

- number of nouns;

- number of noun phrases;

- number of negated words;

- number of main clauses;

- number of relative clauses;

- number of appositive clauses;

- number of noun and verb participial phrases; and

- number of other types of subordinate clauses.

If a simplified sentence contains too many of these, it could be an indication that the simplification system could not reduce its complexity to a desirable degree.

Readability Features

The readability of a sentence can be described as the degree of ease with which it can be read and understood. Readability metrics have been used as a way of determining whether or not a text would pose a challenge to a certain target audience [Kincaid et al., 1975, McLaughlin, 1969, Taylor, 1953]. Because of their inherently strong correlation with simplicity, readability measures can potentially help TS QE approaches in quantifying simplicity.

Nisioi and Nauze [2016] present a QE system that employs some statistics that can be extracted with the Flesch-Kincaid readability framework [Kincaid et al., 1975]. The features extracted are:

- the Flesch-Kincaid readability score of the simplification;

- the minimum age at which one is expected to be able to understand the simplification; and

- the U.S.-grade education level for which the simplification is most appropriate.

5.1.4   ARCHITECTURES

Existing architectures devised for sentence-level QE for TS resemble those used for MT. QE for MT could, in theory, be adapted for TS by using a different feature set that explicitly encompasses grammaticality, meaning preservation and simplicity, either in isolation, or jointly.

Two types of architectures have been used to construct QE approaches for TS: non-sequential and sequential, as introduced in Section 2.5. Due to the flexibility of modern ML algorithms, sequential and non-sequential architectures can be used to create both regressors, which predict continuous quality scores, and classifiers, which predict discrete values. In what follows we focus on the ML algorithms and metrics that have been successfully incorporated in these architectures for TS QE.

Non-Sequential Approaches

Non-sequential approaches are the most widely used in TS QE. Some of the most successful approaches in the QATS 2016 shared task on sentence-level QE for TS use random forests [Štajner et al., 2016], SVM, multi-layer perceptron [Paetzold and Specia, 2016b], and ensembles of multiple algorithms [Nisioi and Nauze, 2016]. These non-sequential models represent the winning submissions for grammaticality, meaning preservation, simplicity, and overall quality.

Sequential Approaches

Sequential approaches for sentence-level QE are those that exploit the fact that the input sentence is actually a sequence of words. Two types of sequential approaches have been explored for this task: linear RNN models and tree-based RNN models.

The few sequential approaches that were submitted to the QATS 2016 shared task performed very well. Paetzold and Specia [2016b] trained RNN regressors that predict the quality not of a sentence, but rather its n-grams. These models are used to predict the quality scores of all n-grams in both the original and simplified sentences. One model is trained for each quality dimension. The scores are then combined through averaging.

Figure 5.3 illustrates how this approach works. First, all n-grams (bigrams in the example) are extracted from both the original and simplified sentences. Each n-gram is then transformed into a sequence of word embeddings that are passed onto a linear unidirectional RNN. The RNN predicts an individual quality score for each n-gram. The resulting scores are then averaged in order to produce a final continuous quality score, which is then transformed into a discrete quality score that can be used in a classification setting. To train these models, the quality score

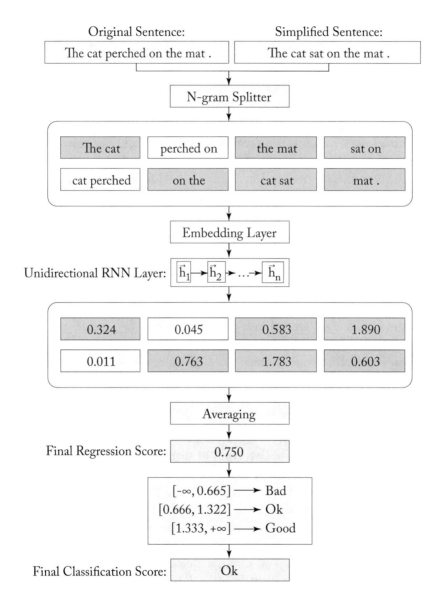

Figure 5.3: **Architecture of the SimpleNets approach** [Paetzold and Specia, 2016b].

of the simplified sentences in the training set is extrapolated to all of its n-grams. This approach attains the highest accuracy scores for overall quality prediction.

The other sequential approach for TS QE was introduced by Nisioi and Nauze [2016]. This sentence-level QE approach consists of an ensemble that combines multiple models, one of which is a sequential tree LSTM model [Tai et al., 2015]. Tree LSTM are a nonlinear type of RNN that receives trees instead of sequences as input. Rather than connecting nodes linearly, like most RNN approaches do, nodes are connected based on the structure of the trees that they receive as input. Figure 5.4 illustrates the difference between a typical linear RNN model and a tree LSTM.

The tree LSTMs approach [Nisioi and Nauze, 2016] takes as input embedding representations of the nodes in the dependency parses of the original and simplified sentences, and produce as output a discrete "good"/"bad" quality label. This label is then used by an ensemble model to produce both continuous and discrete quality scores. The ensemble approach, which we describe in more detail in Section 5.1.6, obtains the highest correlation with grammaticality, simplicity, and overall quality scores in the QATS 2016 shared task. For meaning preservation, they achieve the second highest correlation scores (0.585).

5.1.5   EVALUATION

The QATS 2016 shared task on sentence-level QE for TS covers both classification and regression variants. The datasets are composed of a set of original sentences accompanied by their respective simplification, and one "good"/"ok"/"bad" score for grammaticality, meaning preservation, simplicity and overall quality. Since the "good"/"ok"/"bad" labels are of discrete nature, participants could devise classification approaches for the task. In addition, a numeric representation for these labels was created:

- "good" → 2,

- "ok" → 1, and

- "bad" → 0.

The classification and regression settings were evaluated using metrics previously described in Section 3.6. For classification, the metrics used include accuracy, weighted f-measure, precision, and recall. For regression approaches, Pearson's r correlation coefficient is used, along with MAE and RMSE.

5.1.6   STATE-OF-THE-ART RESULTS

Based on the results reported for the QATS 2016 shared task, two approaches obtained top performance ranks across all quality properties: the random forest classifiers in Štajner et al. [2016] and the hybrid regressors in Nisioi and Nauze [2016]. While the latter achieved the highest weighted F-score values in the classification setting for all quality properties (grammaticality,

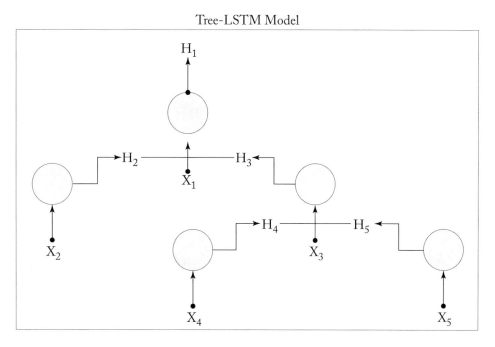

Figure 5.4: Difference between a linear RNN model and a tree LSTM model.

meaning preservation, simplicity, and overall), the former achieved the highest Pearson's *r* correlation coefficient in the regression setting for grammaticality, simplicity, and overall quality.

The Random Forest Classifier Approach

The architecture of the approach in Štajner et al. [2016] is illustrated in Figure 5.5. It follows that of a typical non-sequential QE system. Given an input simplification, two sets of features are first extracted, both of which are MT-inspired:

- **QuEst++ baseline features:** the 17 baseline features for sentence-level QE for MT [Specia et al., 2013]; and

- **MT metrics:** a set of 22 MT evaluation metrics scores, such as BLEU, Meteor, TER, etc.

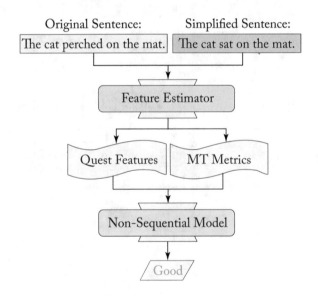

Figure 5.5: Architecture of the Štajner et al. [2016] non-sequential approach.

The features are then passed as input to a non-sequential ML algorithm that learns a model to classify the simplification using the "good"/"ok"/"bad" label set of the shared task. Eight ML algorithms are used in the experiments. Random forest classifiers prove to be the most effective, achieving the highest weighted F-measure scores for grammaticality, simplicity, and overall quality. For meaning preservation, the logistic regression model is the best.

This is a simple and effective approach. Its main limitation is the fact that it relies heavily on a large set of 39 features. While some of the QuEst++ baseline features can be calculated rather efficiently, many of the MT evaluation metrics cannot. Random forests and non-sequential models alike tend to work well when the training sets available are small, which is the case for the QATS 2016 shared task. However, as indicated in Section 2.5, non-sequential models have difficulty exploiting important structural clues such as long-distance word relationships. We believe the performance of non-sequential models would not likely hold against sequential models as TS QE datasets grow in size.

The Hybrid Regressor Approach
Nisioi and Nauze [2016] introduce a sophisticated regression approach for TS QE. It achieved the highest Pearson's *r* correlation coefficient with human-produced labels for almost all quality properties in the QATS 2016 shared task. This is a hybrid approach for regression that combines a sequential tree LSTM model with a swarm optimization ensemble of various types of metrics and models. The approach is illustrated in Figure 5.6.

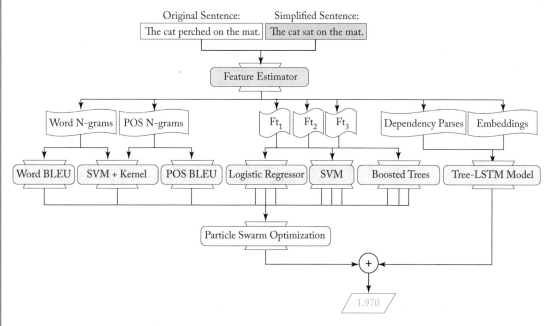

Figure 5.6: **Architecture of the** Nisioi and Nauze [2016] **hybrid approach.**

The feature extractor produces n-grams, POS n-grams, dependency parses, word embeddings, and three other feature sets:

- **Ft_1:** TF-IDF values for words and POS tags of the simplified sentence;

- **Ft_2:** TF-IDF values for words and POS tags of the original and the simplified sentence; and

- **Ft_3:** numerical features extracted from the original and simplified sentences, such as readability scores, number of chunks, etc.

Using these features, various approaches are used to produce 12 types of estimators:

- BLEU score estimators that calculate either the word or the POS tag n-gram precision between the original and simplified sentence;

- logistic regressors, SVM classifiers, and gradient boosted tree classifiers trained with each of the feature sets: Ft_1, Ft_2, or Ft_3; and

- an SVM classifier trained with string kernels that calculates the similarity between the word and POS tag n-grams of the original and simplified sentences.

The supervised models are trained over the QATS 2016 shared task data using the appropriate regression/classification label set depending on the model. The quality label q_f resulting from the combination of these 12 estimators is produced by the weighted sum of all 12 quality estimates, with weights learned from the training set using a particle swarm optimization method.

The output of this ensemble is combined with the quality label produced by a sequential tree LSTM classification model, which was introduced in Section 5.1.4. The tree LSTM model takes as input the original and simplified sentences as two sequences of word embeddings. It passes these embedding representations to a tree-structured set of LSTM nodes, which in turn produces a discrete quality label for the simplification in question.

Standard averaging is used to combine the quality label from the ensemble and tree LSTM model. At the end of the process, a continuous quality label is produced, making this a regression approach. The highest performing variant of this approach achieves first place in all quality dimensions except meaning preservation, where it placed second.

This is a good example of a way to use a sequential model (tree LSTM) to complement non-sequential models. The various ensembling techniques proposed in this approach can be very useful for future work in TS QE. One of the main limitations of this approach is its complexity: It includes 13 quality estimation models/metrics, each of which has to be trained and configured individually.

5.2 AUTOMATIC TEXT SUMMARIZATION

Automatic Text Summarization (ATS) is the task of automatically shortening one or more documents while preserving their most important information. When more than one document is used as input for the summarization process, the task is referred to as multi-document summarization (as opposed to single-document summarization). ATS systems are usually classified in the following categories depending on the method used to reduce content [Nenkova and McKeown, 2011].

- **Extractive**: Entire sentences are selected from the input document(s) and assembled in order to produce the summary.

- **Abstractive:** New text is generated by taking entire sentences or parts of sentences and rewriting them where needed.

Another dimension according to which ATS approaches can be classified is whether or not they are **query-focused**, i.e., whether the content of the summary depends on a predefined topic.

The vast majority of work on ATS is on extractive summarization and, consequently, the majority of the evaluation approaches are designed for this type of approach. One important difference from TS and MT is that evaluation for ATS cannot be done at sentence level, since sentences in the summary are usually repetitions from the source document(s). Therefore, they focus on system or document level evaluation and, consequently, the existing work on QE for this task also follows the same approach.

The main aspects to be evaluated in automatically produced summaries are: content preservation, i.e., whether the summary contains the most important information available on the original document(s), and linguistic quality—mainly coherence, i.e., the selected sentences make sense together [Louis and Nenkova, 2013]. Also, similarly to TS, ATS is a monolingual text-to-text transformation that offers more possibilities of comparison between source and target than MT. Although there are initiatives targeting multilingual summarization [Giannakopoulos, 2013, Giannakopoulos et al., 2017, 2015], no quality prediction work has been done for this type of summarization.

Traditional evaluation on ATS uses Recall-Oriented Understudy for Gisting Evaluation (ROUGE) [Lin, 2004, Lin and Hovy, 2003], pyramid [Nenkova et al., 2007], or responsiveness as metrics. Similarly to BLEU, ROUGE is a reference-based metric. However, while BLEU focuses on precision, ROUGE is recall-oriented and measures similarity between sentences by considering the longest common n-gram statistics between a system output sentence and the corresponding reference text. Pyramid is also reference-based, although it is manually defined. Humans annotate summary content units (SCUs) in all the references available. Each SCU will then receive a weight that represents the number of reference summaries in which it appears. Good automatic summaries are expected to show SCUs with higher weights. Both ROUGE and pyramid require multiple references in order to provide reliable scores, with most datasets containing at least four references. Responsiveness is based on human judgements of quality (similar to judgements of fluency and adequacy in MT). Quality is defined in terms of content and linguistic adequacy.

As with manually produced translations, manually produced summaries are time-consuming and expensive and some previous work has explored ways to evaluate summaries without human references. However, the majority of previous work in this direction differs from the idea of QE for MT, since it does not build ML systems in order to predict a target score. Instead, it uses similarity scores (e.g., cosine similarity or Jensen Shannon divergence) between the source document(s) and the automatic summary [Donaway et al., 2000, Saggion et al., 2010, Steinberger and Ježek, 2009]. Since content is probably the most salient and important factor in summary evaluation, such approaches show considerably high correlations with human evaluation (pyramid and responsiveness) [Louis and Nenkova, 2013].

Although similarity-based evaluation is an important step toward reference-free evaluation in ATS, we do not consider this to be a full-fledged QE approach. This would correspond to one particular dimension of quality, which could be used as a feature in a QE model. Our review focuses on techniques that apply ML to generalize features to predict a quality score. To the best of our knowledge, only two studies have explored QE for ATS. In Sections 5.2.1 and 5.2.2 we present each of these studies in terms of features, models, and state-of-the-art performance.

Another related approach is the work by Rankel et al. [2012]. Regression models are trained in order to predict pyramid, responsiveness, or readability. While some of these ideas may be useful for QE, this work still relies on human summaries in order to extract the features for the regression models. Therefore, we do not consider it a QE approach.

5.2.1   THE SUMMARY ASSESSMENT APPROACH

Louis and Nenkova [2013] provide an extensive study on ATS evaluation without human references. They experiment with several similarity metrics as alternatives for pyramid, responsiveness, and ROUGE, and propose a combination of similarity metrics through regression, where the objective is to predict pyramid scores. They also experiment with pseudo-references as features for predicting human judgements for content coverage. In both cases, the evaluated ATS systems are built for multi-document summarization, i.e., given an input instance that contains multiple documents, the task is to generate a single output summary that contains all relevant and non-redundant information.

Features
The features used in the models built to predict pyramid are divided in three groups: distribution similarity, summary likelihood and topic signatures.

- The distribution similarity features compare the word distributions between the input and the summary.

  - **Kullback Leibler (KL) divergence**: KL is calculated between two probability distributions P and Q and measures the information lost when coding instances from P using Q, where Q is an approximation of P. KL is calculated as shown in Equation (5.1), where $p_P(w)$ is the word probability distribution for the input and $p_Q(w)$ is the word probability distribution for the summary:

$$D(P||Q) = \sum_w p_P(w) \log_2 \frac{p_P(w)}{p_Q(w)}. \tag{5.1}$$

Both input-summary and summary-input directions are calculated, since KL is not symmetric.

- **Jensen Shannon (JS) divergence**: JS assumes that the distance between P and Q is not much different from the average of distance from their respective mean distribution. JS is defined in Equation (5.2), where $A = \frac{P+Q}{2}$ is the mean distribution of P and Q and D is calculated using Equation (5.1). Unlike the KL divergence, JS divergence is symmetric and bounded:

$$J(P||A) = \frac{1}{2}[D(P||A) + D(Q||A)]. \tag{5.2}$$

- **Cosine similarity:** Cosine distance is calculated between the TF-IDF vectors of the input and summary. Two variations are used: one where the TF-IDF vector for the input considers all of its words, and another where the TF-IDF vector for the input only considers the topic signature words. For both cases, the TF-IDF vector for the summary uses all words in the summary.

- The summary likelihood features use a model of word probabilities for the input to compute the likelihood of the summary.

  - The unigram summary probability is calculated as

  $$(p_{inp}w_1)^{n_1}(p_{inp}w_2)^{n_2}...(p_{inp}w_r)^{n_r},$$

  where $(p_{inp}w_1)$ is the probability of the summary word w_i in the input and n_i is the frequency of w_i in the summary.

  - The multinomial summary probability is calculated as

  $$\frac{N!}{n_1!n_2!...n_r!}(p_{inp}w_1)^{n_1}(p_{inp}w_2)^{n_2}...(p_{inp}w_r)^{n_r},$$

  where N is the total number of words in the summary.

- Topic signatures is the set of the most descriptive and topical words in the input, according to a log-likelihood test. The topic signature features are:

  - proportion of the summary that is composed by the input topic signatures, and
  - percentage of the input topic signatures shared by the summary.

Pseudo-references are explored in a similar way to Albrecht and Hwa [2008]. They are selected from a corpus of various ATS system outputs with quality scores given by humans. The outputs of two best, two mediocre, and two worst systems are taken. For each system in the test set, unigram, bigram, trigram, and fourgram ROUGE scores are calculated between the system and each pseudo-reference group (best, mediocre, or worst) and used as features.

QE Models

For building the model that predicts pyramid scores, the distribution similarity, summary likelihood and topic signature features are combined using a linear regression method, having the pyramid scores as labels. The TAC2009 corpus[4] was used as the evaluation dataset, while the TAC2008 corpus[5] is used as the development set. TAC 2009 has 44 inputs, where each input has 10 documents and 53 system outputs. TAC2008 has 48 inputs, with 10 documents each, and 58 system outputs.

The datasets from the DUC2002, DUC2003, DUC2004, and DUC2005 conferences[6] are used for experiments with pseudo-references. The ROUGE-based features are fed to a linear regression algorithm to learn a model that aims to predict the manually assigned content coverage score for each summary in the test set. In other words, the label to predict is a measure of how much of the content of a single reference is represented in the automatic summary. Cross-validation is employed where the summaries from one system in the test set are used for testing the model, while the summaries from the remaining systems are used for training the model. The predicted scores in each interaction of the cross-validation process are averaged for each document in order to compose the final score.

Evaluation

For evaluating the models to predict pyramid scores, two types of metrics are used.

- **Macro (system-level evaluation):** Ranks generated by the automatic metrics are compared with ranks produced by manual evaluation at ATS system level in terms of Spearman's ρ rank correlation coefficient.

- **Micro (summary-level evaluation):** Ranks are predicted for each document, and the comparison between predicted and manual scores is also performed at document level. The evaluation represents a percentage of automatically generated ranks that achieved significant correlation with the manual rank ($p < 0.05$).

For the test set (TAC2009 data) at the macro level, the regression model shows higher Spearman's ρ correlation (0.77) with ranks produced by true pyramid than JS (0.74). However, when the predicted ranks are compared against responsiveness ranks, JS shows higher Spearman's ρ scores (0.67 and 0.70, respectively). At the micro level, the regression model is worse than JS in terms of correlations with pyramid and responsiveness.

The results for the models using pseudo-references are evaluated in terms of the Spearman's ρ rank correlation coefficient between the predicted scores for content coverage and their corresponding human judgements. For DUC2001 and DUC2003, the highest correlation scores are found when the set of two mediocre systems was used for pseudo-references. For DUC2002,

---

[4]https://tac.nist.gov/2009
[5]https://tac.nist.gov/2008
[6]http://www-nlpir.nist.gov/projects/duc/data.html

the highest correlation is found when the set of two worst systems is used for pseudo-references. Finally, for DUC2004 and DUC2005 the highest correlation is achieved when the set of two best systems is used for pseudo-references. This indicates that the type of system output that should be used for pseudo-references is very dependent on the evaluation dataset.

The focus of Louis and Nenkova [2013] is not on regression-based models, but rather on understanding the contribution of different features for the problem. Nevertheless, this work represents the first QE approach to ATS. The regression models predicting pyramid are not consistently better than individual similarity-based metrics between input and summary, such as JS. However, this may be because only similarity-based features are used to built the QE models and thus not all quality dimensions of summaries are explored. More informed models that include more varied features (including those derived from pseudo-references) could present better results. The pseudo-reference-based models could also be extended by combining other features to the ROUGE scores, similarly to what has been done for MT.

5.2.2   THE SUMMARY RANKING APPROACH

In Singh and Jin [2016] a QE ranking framework is proposed for ATS. The motivation is to avoid the need for human references and to take advantage of features that combine different dimensions of summary quality in a prediction model. While traditional ATS evaluation focuses on content overlap only, this framework includes coherence, topical relevance, and other informativeness features to build a QE model. Similar to Louis and Nenkova [2013], the ATS systems evaluated are built for multi-document summarization.

Features
The feature sets are split into three groups.

- **Informativeness features:**
  - **IDF (inverse document frequency):** This is calculated by averaging the IDF for all words in the summary, using frequency information from the entire corpus.
  - **Concreteness:** The MRC database is used to extract the concreteness values for the words in the summary.
  - **Pseudo-summary similarity:** The first paragraph from each document in an input are combined to form an artificial pseudo-reference. This pseudo-reference is then compared to the summary by generating bag-of-words vectors for the two versions and then computing the cosine similarity between them.
  - **SumBasic:** The average weight of all sentences in the summary is measured based on a method proposed by Nenkova and Vanderwende [2005].
  - **Input dependent:** Given an input, these features measure the relevance of a summary. The frequency of the input terms that appear in the summary and the cosine similarity between bag-of-words vectors of the input and the summary are taken as features.

- **Named entities frequency:** A weight is given to the named entities that appear in a summary according to their importance in the documents of the input.

- **N-gram:** The n-gram (unigram or bigram) similarity between the documents in the input and the summary is measured.

- **Coherence features:** LSA is used to measure the coherence of a summary according to a semantic space model built with all the documents in an input. The LSA matrix is built with the documents in the input and decomposed using the first 15 dimensions. The sentences in the summary are then mapped to a vector in the LSA matrix. The similarity between all possible sentence pairs is computed using cosine similarity. The mean and standard deviation are taken as features.

- **Topic features:** LDA is used to extract topical features, with 20 topics for each input. The top 100 words for each topic are used to calculate the topic similarity. A topic-summary distribution for all topics is taken as a feature.

QE Model

The DUC dataset[7] is used to train the QE system. This dataset for multi-document summarization has 50 inputs, where each input has between 25 and 50 documents that share the same topic. Each input has between 30 and 40 system outputs. Outputs were manually annotated for responsiveness and linguistic quality, which serve as labels for QE.

A classification QE model is built using SVM. The objective is to classify pairs of summaries using either predicted responsiveness or predicted linguistic quality in order to derive ranks for the summaries. For instance, if responsiveness is used as the metric, the label is 1 if $R_1 > R_2$ or 0 if $R_2 < R_1$, where R_1 and R_2 are the responsiveness scores of the summaries from system S_1 and S_2, respectively.

A regression model using SVM is also proposed. The model first predicts the quality score (responsiveness or linguistic quality) for each summary, instead of classifying the summary pairs. The pairwise ranking is then derived following the same approach.

Responsiveness is defined using a *Likert* score varying between 1 (least responsive) to 5 (most responsive). Linguistic quality encompasses four dimensions: non-redundancy, referential clarity, focus and structure, and coherence. Each dimension also varies from 1 to 5. One QE model is built for each dimension.

Evaluation

The DUC dataset used contains human and automatically generated summaries. To train the model with the features and configurations defined in the previous sections, different versions of the data are used: "human" (only human summaries), "human and machine" (human summaries and automatic summaries together), and "machine" (only automatic summaries). One question

---

[7]http://www-nlpir.nist.gov/projects/duc/data.html

is whether the QE model is able to differentiate between human and automatic summaries ("human vs. machine"). In addition, the analysis distinguishes cases "with ties", i.e., when human scores are the same for two summaries, and "without ties", where ties are discarded. Accuracy is used to evaluate the classifiers.

When the quality label is responsiveness, the QE model that incorporates all features is better at predicting scores for the "human" subset than for the "machine" subset, in both "with ties" and "without ties" settings. Results for "human and machine" are higher than for "human" and "machine". The regression model outperforms all alternative models when responsiveness is predicted.

When predicting linguistic quality, results are better for prediction "without ties". Structure and coherence are the dimensions with the highest accuracy in both scenarios. Conversely, non-redundancy shows the worst accuracy in the "with ties" configuration, while for "without ties" focus shows the worst accuracy.

Singh and Jin [2016] explore QE for ATS in more details than the previous work of Louis and Nenkova [2013]. The models built for predicting each quality dimension use different feature types, including advanced features that measures coherence and topics. A potential improvement could be the use of feature selection approaches for defining the best features for each quality dimension. Another interesting point to be explored is the prediction of all dimensions using a single model.

5.3   GRAMMATICAL ERROR CORRECTION

Grammatical Error Correction (GEC) consists in automatically correcting grammar mistakes in an input sentence. Similar to ATS and TS, GEC is a monolingual text-to-text transformation application, where the output is also natural language and, therefore, there are many possible correct alternatives. Most work has focused on automatically correcting grammatical errors in essays produced by second language learners (i.e., non-native speakers of a language).

Traditional evaluation work in this area, which is summarized in the efforts at two CoNLL shared tasks [Ng et al., 2014, 2013], use reference-based metrics to evaluate the results of GEC systems. In particular, the reference-based metrics used for this task are: M^2 (MaxMatch) [Dahlmeier and Ng, 2012], I-measure [Felice and Briscoe, 2015], and GLEU [Napoles et al., 2015]. M^2 computes an F-measure over a set of phrase-level edits that leads to maximum overlap with references. I-measure calculates the accuracy of alignments between source, reference, and GEC output. Finally, GLEU is an n-gram matching metric, similar to BLEU, that penalizes n-grams that appear in the original and in the GEC output, but not in the references.

However, reference-based approaches have similar drawbacks to those that occur in other NLP tasks: They require references and it is important that these represent the collection of all possible correct outputs. Therefore, QE is also an appealing evaluation framework for GEC systems.

So far, two papers have addressed QE for GEC and we describe both in what follows. Similar to Section 5.2, here we focus on features, models and evaluation.

5.3.1   THE "THERE'S NO COMPARISON" APPROACH

Napoles et al. [2016] explore ways to rank GEC systems without relying on human references. For this purpose, individual reference-less metrics are studied and ML models are built in order to predict grammaticality.

Two metrics for ranking GEC systems that rely on counting grammatical errors are computed using two tools that detect grammatical errors: e-rater[8]—ER—and Language Tool[9]—LT. The final metric score is calculated as $1 - \frac{\#errors}{\#tokens}$. These two metrics alone show high correlation with human-produced ranks. In fact, ER shows the same Spearman ρ as GLEU (calculated using human references). These reference-less metrics, together with reference-based GLEU, I-measure and M^2 are compared to the QE model in the evaluation.

Features

For prediction, Napoles et al. [2016] experiment with a "linguistic feature-based model". This is a QE model built using features from the sentences in the system output and an ML algorithm to predict grammaticality. QE is done, therefore, at sentence level, with grammaticality as label. The following features are explored.

- **Misspelled words:** This includes number of misspelled words (n_{miss}), proportion of misspelled words ($\frac{n_{miss}}{n}$), and $\log(n_{miss} + 1)$ (where n is the total number of words). Misspelled words are identified using a dictionary.

- **N-gram counts:** For each sentence in the output, counts of its n-grams are obtained from the English Gigaword corpus [Parker et al., 2011], with $n = 1...3$. The following features are then computed, where S_n are the n-grams of order n for a given sentence:

   - $\sum_{s \in S_n} \frac{\log(count(s)+1)}{||S_n||}$,
   - $\max_{s \in S_n} \log(count(s) + 1)$,
   - $\min_{s \in S_n} \log(count(s) + 1)$.

- **LM:** Average log-probability of sentence and number of out-of-vocabulary words. The LM model is trained on the English Gigaword corpus.

- **Link grammar parser:** A binary feature that indicates whether at least one complete linkage was found for a sentence, according to the Link Grammar Parser.[10]

---

[8]https://www.ets.org/erater/about
[9]https://www.languagetool.org
[10]http://www.link.cs.cmu.edu/link/

- **PCFG parsing:** The parser score for the sentence (normalized by the sentence length), a binary feature that indicates whether or not the top node of the parse tree is sentential; and the number of "dep" relations in the dependency parse tree ("dep" relations are underspecified and may be a sign of grammatical errors).

QE Model

GUG, the dataset used for training Heilman et al. [2014], consists of 3,129 sentences extracted from essays produced by non-native speakers of English. These sentences were annotated using a *Likert* scale of $[1 - 4]$, where 4 means perfect grammaticality. The QE model is built by using ridge regression, with the hyperparameter α tuned via 5-fold cross-validation on the training data.

Evaluation

The CoNLL-2014 Shared Task dataset [Ng et al., 2014] is used for evaluating the QE model. This corpus contains 12 GEC system outputs for each of the 50 essays in the test set (1,312 sentences). In addition, human ranks are available for this dataset. The predicted grammaticality scores are evaluated by means of Spearman's ρ rank correlation coefficient between them and the human ranks. The predicted scores can produce ranks that show higher correlation with human scores than reference-based I-measure or M^2. However, the model has worse correlation with human scores than reference-based GLEU and reference-less ER or LT.

Although the focus of Napoles et al. [2016] is not to build prediction models, the first QE model proposed and the comparisons against traditional reference-based and simple reference-less metrics may be useful for future work in the area. In fact, the next section presents an extension of this approach.

5.3.2 FLUENCY AND MEANING PRESERVATION

Asano et al. [2017] extend the work of Napoles et al. [2016] by including fluency and meaning preservation as evaluation dimensions in addition to grammaticality. Each dimension of quality is extracted separately and then linearly combined into a single score in which weights are learned for each criteria using data from an annotated corpus.

Features

For extracting grammaticality information, a QE model similar to the one built by Napoles et al. [2016] is used. In addition to the features presented in the previous section, the number of errors detected by the Language Tool is also included in the feature set. In addition, the LM was trained using the Gigaword corpus and the TOEFL11 dataset [Blanchard et al., 2013]. The model, represented here after by $S_G(\hat{y})$, where $\hat{y}$ is a sentence output by a GEC system, was also trained with the GUG dataset, with grammaticality as the quality label.

For measuring fluency, they consider Equation (5.3):

$$S_F(\hat{y}) = \frac{\log P_m(\hat{y}) - \log P_u(\hat{y})}{|\hat{y}|}, \tag{5.3}$$

where $\hat{y}$ is a sentence output by a GEC system, $|\hat{y}|$ is the sentence length, $P_m(\hat{y})$ is the language model probability of sentence $\hat{y}$ and $P_u(\hat{y})$ is the unigram probability. The LM is trained with the British National Corpus and Wikipedia data.

Meaning preservation is measured by calculating Meteor between the original and the automatically corrected sentences. For a sentence output by a GEC system ($\hat{y}$) and an original sentence (x), Meteor is calculated as shown in Equation (5.4), where $t = 0.85$, $P = \frac{m(\hat{y}_c, x_c)}{|\hat{y}_c|}$, $R = \frac{m(\hat{y}_c, x_c)}{|x_c|}$. The parameters $\hat{y}_c$ and x_c represent the content words in $\hat{y}$ and x, respectively. The function $m(\hat{y}_c, x_c)$ defines the number of content word matches between $\hat{y}_c$ and x_c, considering inflections, synonyms, and misspellings:

$$S_M(\hat{y}, x) = \frac{P \cdot R}{t \cdot P + (1 - t) \cdot R'}. \tag{5.4}$$

QE Model
The $S_G(\hat{y})$, $S_F(\hat{y})$, and $S_M(\hat{y}, x)$ scores are linearly combined as shown in Equation (5.5), where the sum of α, β, and γ is 1 and all the scores range between 0 and 1:

$$Score(\hat{y}, x) = \alpha S_G(\hat{y}) + \beta S_F(\hat{y}) + \gamma S_M(\hat{y}, x). \tag{5.5}$$

The parameters α, β, and γ were learned using the JFLEG dataset [Napoles et al., 2017]. This dataset has a set of student essays, and for each essay the outputs of four GEC systems and a human score are provided.[11]

Evaluation
The CoNLL-2014 Shared Task dataset is also used for evaluating the final combined quality score, $S_F(\hat{y})$, in the same way as Napoles et al. [2016]. Rankings produced by $Score(\hat{y}, x)$ show a stronger correlation with human scores than GLEU in terms of Spearman's ρ rank correlation coefficient. By considering only individual quality dimensions, $S_M(\hat{y}, x)$ is the only dimension that, on its own, does not show strong correlation with human scores. However, when combined with $S_F(\hat{y})$, $S_M(\hat{y}, x)$ boosts the correlation score, which does not occur when only $S_G(\hat{y})$ and $S_M(\hat{y}, x)$ are combined.

The dataset produced by Sakaguchi et al. [2016] is also used for evaluation. This dataset is a version of the CoNLL-2014 dataset, with minimal edits, i.e., the minimum edits to make the sentence grammatical, and fluent edits, i.e., the edits need to make the sentence fluent. Both minimal and fluent edit versions are produced by humans. This dataset is used to determine

---

[11]The weights learned were $\alpha = 0.07$, $\beta = 0.83$ and $\gamma = 0.10$.

whether $Score(\hat{y}, x)$ selects fluent edits over minimal edits. $Score(\hat{y}, x)$ is shown to prefer fluent sentences, whilst GLEU and M² prefer sentences with minimal edits.

In summary, this work is an important extension of Napoles et al. [2016] toward a full QE framework for GEC. However, a QE model for GEC may benefit from other feature types, mainly for grammaticality and meaning preservation. A framework that jointly learns all dimensions at once may also bring additional improvements to the task.

5.4   AUTOMATIC SPEECH RECOGNITION

An ASR system takes as input an audio signal containing speech segments and attempts to produce an accurate transcription of it. The subsentence-level variant of QE for MT was actually inspired by work on word- and phrase-level confidence estimation for ASR. As discussed in Section 2.2, in word-level confidence estimation for ASR one aims to predict how confident a given ASR system is that a certain segment of an audio signal can be translated into a certain word. Jiang [2005] describes and compares several word-level confidence estimation approaches, and highlight the fact that most of them produce confidence estimates in unsupervised fashion, which is different from the general approach used for QE of MT.

Recently, however, Negri et al. [2014] introduced a supervised word-level QE approach for ASR that aims at estimating the quality of transcriptions following a standard QE framework. Their approach takes as input both the audio signal and the transcription of a given segment produced by an ASR system, and produces as output the segment's estimated Word Error Rate (WER). They use a non-sequential regression model trained using SVMs or extremely rrandomized trees with data labeled for WER, which is calculated by comparing a system transcription with a manually created reference transcription. As features they use language and acoustic model probabilities, Mel Frequency Cepstral coefficients and energy measures from the audio signal, word-type counts from the transcription, and hybrid features that combine audio and transcription through alignment.

Their model proved more effective than a strong baseline and showed that predicting the quality of audio transcriptions is feasible.

5.5   NATURAL LANGUAGE GENERATION

Natural Language Generation (NLG) approaches aim to generate text in human language [Reiter and Dale, 2000] from a range of structured representations. Different from text-to-text transformations, such as MT or ATS, NLG systems receive as input structured representations that are more abstract than language and generally intend to express the meaning of the text to be generated. Therefore, they perform data-to-text transformations [Gatt and Krahmer, 2018]. Such abstract representations can take different forms, for example structured knowledge bases, meaning representations, or even images.

Since the input can vary significantly, it is difficult to create a single evaluation framework for NLG that generalizes across representations. We refer the reader to Gatt and Krahmer [2018] for more details on NLG evaluation. In general, NLG is evaluated based on human judgments (e.g., fluency, adequacy, or readability) or reference-based metrics (e.g., BLEU, ROUGE, TER or pyramid). However, the fact that NLG can assume different inputs and that the size of the output can also vary considerably, producing a representative set of references is even more problematic in NLG than in other tasks. QE can be thus used to enable task-based evaluation without reference texts.

QE for NLG is related to work on predicting stylistic characteristics in order to improve the performance of NLG systems [Dethlefs et al., 2014, Mairesse and Walker, 2011, Paiva and Evans, 2005]. Stylistic prediction consists in automatically identifying to which degree a text encompasses a given stylistic realization. For example, Dethlefs et al. [2014] predict the degree of *politeness*, *colloquialism*, and *naturalness* of NLG system outputs. Although stylistic realizations can be seen as aspects of quality, existing work has not addressed them as such and, therefore, we to not detail it in this book. In what follows, we describe the only two approaches we are aware of that address quality prediction for NLG.

5.5.1 THE QE RANKING APPROACH

Dušek et al. [2017] propose an approach for QE of NLG using neural networks. An RNN-based model is trained to estimate the quality of the output of an NLG system by directly comparing such an output to the corresponding input meaning representation, as we explain below.

Data
To obtain labeled data, the outputs of the three following NLG systems are manually evaluated by crowdsourcing.

- LOLS: a system based on imitation learning [Lampouras and Vlachos, 2016].

- RNNLG: a system using RNNs [Wen et al., 2015].

- TGen: a perceptron-guided tree generation system [Dušek and Jurčíček, 2015].

Each crowd worker received two randomly selected system outputs and the corresponding source meaning representation. They were asked to assess the overall quality of both system outputs using a 1–6 *Likert* scale, where 6 is the highest score for quality. An output produced by an NLG system is a segment composed of one or two sentences. These automatically generated outputs are evaluated by at least three annotators. The final quality scores for each segment is the median of all annotations. Three datasets are used.

- BAGEL [Mairesse et al., 2010]: 404 segments about restaurants.

- SFRest [Wen et al., 2015]: around 5,000 segments also from the restaurant domain.

• SFHot [Wen et al., 2015]: around 5,000 segments from the hotel domain.

The input for NLG approaches are meaning representations in the form of dialogue acts (DA). A DA is composed by the main DA type (e.g., *inform*, *request*), optional slots (e.g., *food*, *location*), and values (e.g., *Chinese*). In the approach by Dušek et al. [2017], the DAs are converted into triplets (DA type—slot—value), where the same DA type can be repeated several times according to the number of slots/values associated with it. In order to prevent sparsity, delexicalization is used where, for example, *Chinese* is replaced by *X-food* in both input and output occurrences.

QE Model

The RNN model for QE as two encoders, one for the input DA and another for the target segment, where each encoder uses a Gated Recurrent Unit (GRU). The GRU encoders are followed by two fully connected `tahn` layers that use the final hidden states of both encoders as input. The last layer in the architecture, a linear layer, predicts a number in 1–6 that represents the quality score.

Dušek et al. [2017] also experiment with augmenting the training data. More data is generated by introducing errors into system outputs or human references and adapting the quality score accordingly. When available, human references are considered as segments with the highest quality score (6). For each error introduced, the quality score of the segment is deducted by 1. If the segment has a score higher or equal to 5.5, the first error lowers the score to 4 and, from the second error onward, 1 is deducted from the quality scores.

The neural network is trained for 500 epochs with the aim to maximize Pearson's r and Spearman's ρ correlation scores on a validation set. The model showing the best correlation for both measurements is then selected. For experiments with data augmentation, the QE system is trained for 20 epochs with all the data. The best parameters are used to initialize the training with only the original data.

Evaluation

In order to evaluate the QE systems, Dušek et al. [2017] use Pearson's r correlation coefficient, Spearman's ρ rank correlation coefficient, MAE, and RMSE. Dušek et al. [2017] also compare the results of the QE systems with traditional reference-based metrics: BLEU, Meteor, ROUGE, and CIDEr [Vedantam et al., 2015].

The QE systems evaluated differ mainly regarding the type and amount of data used (i.e., whether or not data augmentation was used). All proposed systems outperform the reference-based metrics. The best system is built with all the data available (original and augmented data, including human references). Such a system achieves a Pearson's r score of 0.354, a Spearman's ρ score of 0.287, a MAE of 0.909, and a RMSE of 1.208. The values for MAE and RMSE are significantly better than the MAE and RMSE of a mean baseline (MAE = 1.013 and RMSE = 1.233).

Dušek et al. [2017] also experiment with out-of-domain and cross-system prediction scenarios. Although the QE systems seems to perform well for the cross-system case, out-of-domain data does not improve over a system trained with only a small amount of in-domain data.

5.5.2   QE FOR BROWSE PAGES

Ueffing et al. [2018] propose QE models for evaluating the quality of automatically generated titles of *browse pages* for eCommerce websites. A browse page is an intermediate webpage that groups various items together (e.g., smart phones). Browse pages contain a summary description of such items that share some, but not all, characteristics (e.g., smart phones from different brands). The content of a browse page can be viewed as slot-value pairs (similarly to the realization of *food* as a slot and *Chinese* as value in the previous section). More specifically, Ueffing et al. [2018] describe the need for QE in NLG at companies like eBay, where the content of browse pages refers to products for sale and there are millions of browse pages available in various languages. Examples of slots are *color* and *brand*, while the corresponding values could be *white* and *Apple*, respectively, and the *category* could be *cell phones and smart phones*. The motivation for QE in this task is that different browse pages should encode different features and, therefore, should be represented by different titles. In a large eCommerce website, generating titles manually is unfeasible not only due to the amount of data, but also because titles may be needed in different languages. Therefore, approaches to automatically generate such titles are desired and, consequently, automatic approaches for evaluating the quality of the titles, such as QE approaches, are needed.

Data
The original data for automatically generating titles corresponds of a *category* name followed by a number of slot-values pairs. For QE, titles automatically generated by a rule-based system are also available and manually annotated according to the following classes.

1. **Good quality**: No issues.

2. **Acceptable quality**: Minor issues.

3. **Medium quality**: Issues that impact understandability.

4. **Bad quality**: Major issues (e.g., incorrect brand names).

Ueffing et al. [2018] simplify this annotation to a binary decision: 1 and 2 receive the "ok" label and 3 and 4 receive the "bad" label. The experiments are performed with titles generated for English.

Artificial data is also used in order to augment examples for the type "bad" (only around 1% of the titles were labeled with class 4). Ueffing et al. [2018] selected approximately 29,000 browse pages containing *brand* slots from the data and changed the reference titles for such browse pages, misspelling the brand name. For training, around 380,000 browse pages were used, while for testing, 2 test sets of 500 browse pages each were used.

Three title generation systems were evaluated:

- a rule-based approach with a manually created grammar;

- a hybrid generation approach that combines rule-based and SMT techniques; and

- an automatic post-editing (APE) approach where the titles are first generated using a rule-based approach and then post-edited using an SMT model.

QE Model

Two ML algorithms are explored by Ueffing et al. [2018]: random forests and Siamese networks. Random forests ensemble multiple decision trees for classification based on a set of features. Three types of features are used.

- MTQE: features inspired by those from QE for MT, e.g., LM probability.

- BP: features specifically developed for dealing with information from the browse page metadata, e.g., indicators of incorrect brand names.

- Redundancy: features to capture redundancy in the titles (e.g., word repetition).

Random forest models are built taking each feature set individually and combined. Hyperparameters are optmized with random search for 100 iterations and 5-fold cross-validation. Siamese networks are neural networks composed by two sub-networks that can predict the similarity between paired inputs. In Ueffing et al. [2018], in order to predict how adequate and fluent an automatically produced title is for a given browse page, the sub-networks are two LSTMs—one for the browse pages metadata and another for the title—with tied weights, which implies that both networks perform identical transformations. The output is a similarity score, defined after calculating cosine similarity between the last hidden states of each LSTM.

Evaluation

F1-score per class, weighted F1-score and Matthew's correlation coefficient[12] are used as evaluation metrics. When no artificial data is used, the Siamese network models are only better than random forest models with all features in terms of F1-score of the "ok" class. However, the additional data with more"bad" class cases improves the results of the Siamese network models, which consistently outperform random forrest models according to all metrics.

---

[12]Matthew's correlation coefficient is used to evaluate the quality of binary classification tasks. It is robust for cases where the classes are considerably unbalanced and, therefore, it is a more reliable metric than accuracy for such cases. It can be seen as a discretization of Pearson's r correlation coefficient and it also varies from -1 to 1, where 1 indicates full positive correlation, -1 indicates full negative correlation and 0 represents no correlation.

Ueffing et al. [2018] also report the performance of QE for each title generation system. The best F1-and Matthew's correlation scores were achieved by the rule-based system, followed by the hybrid system.

CHAPTER 6

Final Remarks

QE, as presented in this book, is the task of predicting the quality of a given output of an NLP application without relying on comparisons against manually produced references. More specifically, QE focuses on NLP applications that output natural language. Since there are often multiple correct outputs for these applications, standard evaluation metrics that match system outputs against reference texts are far from reliable. In addition, QE can improve user experience with NLP applications by providing a quality prediction in real-world usage scenarios for which human references are not available. QE models are learned from data using machine learning techniques, which facilitates more flexible modeling of particular relevant quality dimensions according to the respective application scenario.

This book concentrated on QE for MT, since MT is probably the most widely used language output NLP application and, consequently, a considerable amount of work has been done in this field. We covered three levels of prediction.

- **Subsentence-level QE:** A quality score is predicted for each word or phrase.

- **Sentence-level QE:** A quality score is predicted for each given sentence.

- **Document-level QE:** A quality score is predicted for an entire document.

For each prediction level we presented main applications, labels, features, and architectures, as well as evaluation methodologies and state-of-the-art approaches. In general, the most successful approaches use neural models, moving from the traditional focus on feature engineering to that of architecture engineering. Another promising direction is the use of joint models to perform quality prediction and automatic post-editing.

Sentence-level QE is the most popular prediction level, with most current work predicting some representation of post-editing effort. It is usually addressed as a supervised machine learning regression task using a variety of algorithms to induce models from examples of sentence translations annotated with quality labels, e.g., 1–5 *Likert* scores. This prediction level has featured in all shared tasks organized by the WMT annually since 2012 [Bojar et al., 2013, 2014, 2017, 2016, 2015, Callison-Burch et al., 2012]. State-of-the-art approaches use neural methods to learn features and models from relatively small amounts of annotated data in combination with large amounts of source-target language parallel data that is not annotated for quality.

Word-level QE has been receiving more attention recently, with most work predicting binary "good"/"bad" labels, mostly due to the lack of annotated corpora with more fine-grained error annotation. Both sequential and non-sequential algorithms have been used with a large variety of word and contextual features as well as learned representations. An application that can benefit from word-level QE is error detection in a post-editing workflow. This prediction level has featured in the last five editions of the WMT shared tasks. An open challenge with word-level QE is the prediction of more specific types of error levels without depending on large quantities of data annotated for the respective errors. Similarly to sentence-level QE, state-of-the-art methods are based on neural architectures that explore weak supervision, such as parallel data without explicit quality annotations.

Document-level QE was introduced more recently and still suffers from the lack of reliably annotated corpora. This task was organized as a track at WMT15 and WMT16. Existing work predicts absolute scores for a document or relative ranking of translations by one or more systems. Algorithms and features similar to those used for sentence-level prediction are explored. This level is particularly useful for *gisting* purposes, where post-editing is not an option. Annotating a document with a single global quality score that represents more than the aggregation of sentence-level scores is a very challenging task even for humans. The biggest challenge for this prediction level is finding effective labels and annotation protocols. This may in practice only be possible for very short documents.

6.1   FUTURE DIRECTIONS

Thus far, shared tasks as well as the vast majority of published work have built models for the output of statistical- and rule-based MT systems. With neural systems quickly becoming the *de facto* approach to MT, the natural next step is to build models to predict the quality of these systems. This is likely to prove a more difficult challenge for QE: Neural MT systems are based on a strong target LMs component that is primarily responsible for guiding the decoding process to generate translations. As a result, these systems tend to produce translations that are fluent, but in many cases inadequate. In feature-based QE work, LM features are among the strongest in capturing translation quality. These and other fluency indicators are expected to be much less effective for translations produced by neural MT systems. The 2018 edition of the WMT shared task on QE[1] includes neural MT output. The shared task results will provide the first benchmark and certainly open new research avenues on effective QE approaches for this type of translation.

Neural architectures to QE such as the ones discussed in Chapter 2 are likely to predominate among upcoming approaches, given their promising performance and also their flexibility to deal with different granularity levels, as well as to deal with these levels jointly, for example using multi-task learning. An interesting direction that could be exploited using such approaches are general purpose sentence embeddings [Kiros et al., 2015] instead of or in addition to word embeddings, in particular for sentence-level QE. Methods that go beyond sentences to estimate how well a sentence fits a document context also represent a promising direction, especially for document-level QE. Another promising direction for document-level QE is to further exploit

---

[1]http://www.statmt.org/wmt18/quality-estimation-task.html

extrinsic quality labels, such as the success in completing a task, for example buying a product based on machine-translated content.

The promising results from addressing QE as a by-product of automatic post-editing [Hokamp, 2017, Martins et al., 2017a] should also be further pursued. Even though fixing MT output is not needed for cases where MT is used for gisting (and the process may actually add errors to the translation), the general idea of treating the problem as that of automatic post-editing could provide good approximations on the proportion of the content that would need to be edited. This may prove more useful for sentence-level QE where, as opposed to word-level QE, the actual words marked as incorrect are not as important, as long as the proportion of words identified as incorrect is close enough to the actual proportion of incorrect words.

Neural approaches tend to require more training data as well as more time (and computational resources) to train models. While some approaches can be pre-trained with unlabeled data [Kim et al., 2017b], they still perform better if more labeled data is available. Strategies to automatically label data at various granularity levels, like it was done for traditional feature-based QE on statistical MT data [Logacheva and Specia, 2015] and recently for quality prediction for automatically generated browse page titles [Ueffing et al., 2018], could be very useful. Finding and labeling negative data, i.e., translations with errors, would be particularly critical, given that good quality translations can be easily taken from instances of human translation. Designing neural QE models that can work on less data (and resources) or better leverage unlabeled data are also important directions.

Another general challenge for QE is the investigation of realistic extrinsic evaluation methodologies with end-users. Very little work has been done toward evaluating the use of QE in real-world settings. For example, it is still not clear how predictions on post-editing effort can be best included in a translation workflow in order to improve productivity and, potentially, reduce costs.

This book also covered work on QE for other language output applications, namely TS, ATS, GEC, ASR, and NLG. These are much more recent endeavours, but interesting results have been reported and we hope that other researchers will consider developing approaches for these and potentially other applications.

6.2   RESOURCES AND TOOLKITS

A non-exhaustive list of resources and toolkits that have been developed for QE—mostly for MT—is presented in this section. We hope that this list can encourage and inspire further research in QE not only for MT but also for other NLP tasks. The following toolkits have been released.

- **deeqQuest** implements neural models for QE at word, sentence and document levels [Ive et al., 2018]. These models include a re-implementation of the POSTECH approach [Kim et al., 2017b] as well as a light-weight approach based on bi-directional RNNs which performs competitively. The models do not require any additional resources other than the QE training data, but parallel (source-reference) data can be used for better results. Available from: `https://github.com/sheffieldnlp/deepQuest`.

- **QuEst++** offers feature extraction, model training, and prediction for word-, sentence-, and document-level QE [Specia et al., 2015]. The feature extraction module was developed in Java and uses several wrappers to access external NLP tools, while for model training, wrappers are provided for use with the Python scikit-learn [Pedregosa et al., 2011] and the CRFSuite [Okazaki, 2007] toolkits. QuEst++ has been used to build the baseline systems for the sentence and document-level tasks at the WMT. Available from: `http://www.quest.dcs.shef.ac.uk/`. The previous version of QuEst++, called QuEst [Specia et al., 2013], was integrated into the Okapi framework [Paetzold et al., 2015].[2] In addition, a graphical interface that uses QuEst, called **QuEst-Online**, is also available: `http://www.quest.dcs.shef.ac.uk/quest_files/Online-QuEst.zip`.

- **Marmot** was developed in Python for feature extraction, model training, and prediction focusing on word- and phrase-level QE [Logacheva et al., 2016b]. This tool relies on NLP and ML libraries available for Python in order to perform feature extraction, model training, and prediction. Marmot can use any classifier in scikit-learn. It can also output features in various formats suitable for other ML tools. Marmot has been used as a baseline system for the word and phrase-level tasks at the WMT. Available from: `https://github.com/qe-team/marmot`.

- **WCE-LIG** was developed in Python for feature extraction, training and prediction for word-level QE [Servan et al., 2015]. For feature extraction, wrappers are used to access externalNLP tools. CRF models can be built by using a wrapper to the Wapiti toolkit [Lavergne et al., 2010]. Available from: `https://github.com/besacier/WCE-LIG`.

- **Qualitative** is a Python tool that supports feature extraction, model training, and prediction for sentence-level QE [Avramidis, 2016]. This tool was mainly designed for sentence-level machine translation ranking and enables an MT system combination on the output of various types of MT systems. Features are extracted using wrappers to access external NLP tools. The ML module supports Orange [Demšar et al., 2004], scikit-learn and MLpython[3] toolkits. Available from: `https://github.com/lefterav/qualitative`.

- **QE::GUI** [Avramidis, 2017] is a graphical interface for Qualitative: Available from: `https://github.com/lefterav/qegui`.

- **Asiya** is a toolkit that was written in Perl to extracts metrics for traditional reference-based MT evaluation and as well as a set of features for sentence- and document-level QE [Giménez and Màrquez, 2010]. Available from: `http://asiya.lsi.upc.edu/`.

---

[2] `http://okapiframework.org/wiki/index.php?title=QuEst_Plugin`
[3] `http://www.dmi.usherb.ca/~larocheh/mlpython/`

Many datasets have been created and used in previous work, including the following.

- The **WMT** annual QE shared tasks datasets 2012–2017. These include a range of language pairs, text domains, MT systems, label types, and granularity of annotations.

  - **WMT12:** Sentence-level scoring for perceived post-editing effort (English-Spanish, news domain).

  - **WMT13:** Sentence-level scoring for HTER and post-editing time (English-Spanish, news domain), sentence-level system selection (German-English and English-Spanish, news domain), and word-level binary and multi-class classification (English-Spanish, news domain).

  - **WMT14:** Sentence-level scoring for perceived post-editing effort (English-Spanish, Spanish-English, English-German and German-English, news domain), sentence-level scoring for HTER and post-editing time (English-Spanish, news domain), and word-level binary and multi-class classification (English-Spanish, Spanish-English, English-German and German-English, news domain).

  - **WMT15:** Sentence-level scoring for HTER (English-Spanish, news domain), word-level binary classification QE (English-Spanish, news domain), and paragraph-level scoring for Meteor (English-German and German-English, news domain).

  - **WMT16:** Sentence-level scoring for HTER (English-German of IT domain), word-level and phrase-level binary classification QE (English-German, IT domain), and document-level scoring for two-stage post-editing effort (English-Spanish, news domain).

  - **WMT17:** Sentence-level scoring for HTER and word-level and phrase-level binary classification (English-German, IT domain and German-English, life sciences domain).

  - **WMT18:** Sentence-level scoring for HTER, word-level and phrase-level 2 and 3-way classification (English-German and English-Czech, IT domain, German-English and English-Latvian, life sciences domain), as well as document-level scoring for average MQM-score (English-French, product title and descriptions). This shared task provides the output of neural MT for English-German, English-Latvian, and English-French. Another novelty is the task of detecting missing words (deletions errors) in the MT output, as well as the corresponding source words.

  Available from the WMT QE shared task webpages: `http://www.statmt.org/wmtx/quality-estimation-task.html`, where x represents a year in $\{12, 13, 14, 15, 16, 17\}$.

- **AUTODESK** is a large dataset (IT domain) containing professional post-edits for sentences machine translated from English into 13 languages, from which HTER can be computed. Available from: `https://autodesk.app.box.com/v/Autodesk-PostEdit ing/folder/2960023815`.

- **LIG** contains English-French sentences in the news domain with post-edits at sentence level [Potet et al., 2012], from which HTER can be computed. Available from: `http: //www-clips.imag.fr/geod/User/marion.potet/index.php?page=download`.

- **TRACE** contains English-French and French-English post-edited sentences including news domains and TED talks [Wisniewski et al., 2013], from which HTER can be computed. Available from: `http://anrtrace.limsi.fr/trace_postedit.tar.bz2`.

- **QT21** is a large dataset of professionally produced post-edits for sentences in the IT (English-German and English-Czech) and life sciences (English-Latvian and German-English) domains. Besides the machine-translated sentences and their post-edited counterparts, this corpus contains other effort indicators logged during post-editing process: post-editing time, keystrokes, and *Likert* scores [Specia et al., 2017]. Available from: `https://lindat.mff.cuni.cz/repository/xmlui/handle/11372/LRT-2390`.

- **EAMT09** is an English-Spanish dataset (Europarl domain) with source sentences translated by four MT systems. The translated sentences were evaluated by professional translators for perceived MT quality [Specia et al., 2009a]. Available from: `http://staffwww .dcs.shef.ac.uk/people/L.Specia/resources/ce_dataset.rar`.

- **EAMT11** contains English-Spanish and French-English sentences (news domain), including post-edited sentences, post-editing time and HTER measurements, and perceived MT quality score following a 1–4-point scale performed by professionals [Specia, 2011]. Available from: `http://staffwww.dcs.shef.ac.uk/people/L.Specia/re sources/datasets_ce_eamt.tar.gz`.

- **WPTP12** is an English-Spanish dataset (news domain) with machine translations from eight MT systems [Koponen et al., 2012]. Post-edited sentences are given along with measurements of post-editing time and HTER. Available from: `http://staffwww.dcs .shef.ac.uk/people/L.Specia/resources/wptp-2012_dataset.tar.gz`.

- **GREG-MT-eval** is a German-English dataset containing documents that were machine translated by four MT systems [Scarton and Specia, 2016]. This dataset contains marks for reading comprehension tests on the machine-translated documents by a number of test takers. Available from: `https://github.com/carolscarton/CREG-MT-eval`.

- **QATS** (for TS) is a dataset with original and automatically simplified English sentences annotated with scores for grammaticality, meaning preservation and simplicity [Štajner et al., 2016]. Available from: `http://qats2016.github.io/shared.html`.

- **DUC** (for ATS) provides various corpora from the shared tasks on ATS of the Document Understanding Conferences (DUC) between 2002 and 2007. Manual and automatic summaries are provided, where the latter are annotated with different types of scores derived from human evaluation. Available under request from: `http://www-nlpir.nist.gov/projects/duc/data.html`.

- **TAC** (for ATS) are datasets from the shared tasks in ATS organized for the Text Analysis Conference (TAC) for the years of 2008, 2009, 2010, 2011, and 2014. For each edition, different types of evaluation scores are available. Available under request from: `https://tac.nist.gov/data/index.html`.

- **GUG** (for GEC) is a dataset with sentences extracted from essays produced by English language learners with *Likert* scores for grammaticality [Heilman et al., 2014]. Available from: `https://github.com/EducationalTestingService/gug-data`.

- **JF-LEG** [Napoles et al., 2017] is an extension of the GUG corpus that contains human corrections and an annotation of perceived correction effort according to a *Likert* scale. Available from: `https://github.com/keisks/jfleg`.

Bibliography

Amal Abdelsalam, Ondřej Bojar, and Samhaa El-Beltagy. 2016. Bilingual embeddings and word alignments for translation quality estimation. In *Proc. of the 1st Conference on Machine Translation*, pages 764–771. DOI: 10.18653/v1/w16-2380 56

Joshua Albrecht and Rebecca Hwa. 2008. The role of pseudo references in MT evaluation. In *Proc. of the 3rd Workshop on Statistical Machine Translation*, pages 187–190. DOI: 10.3115/1626394.1626424. 55, 100

Mandya Angrosh, Tadashi Nomoto, and Advaith Siddharthan. 2014. Lexico-syntactic text simplification and compression with typed dependencies. In *Proc. of the 25th International Conference on Computational Linguistics*, pages 1996–2006. 82

Hiroki Asano, Tomoya Mizumoto, and Kentaro Inui. 2017. Reference-based metrics can be replaced with reference-less metrics in evaluating grammatical error correction systems. In *Proc. of the 8th International Joint Conference on Natural Language Processing*, pages 343–348. 106

Eleftherios Avramidis. 2012. Comparative quality estimation: Automatic sentence-level ranking of multiple machine translation outputs. In *Proc. of the 24th International Conference on Computational Linguistics*, pages 115–132. 49

Eleftherios Avramidis. 2013. Sentence-level ranking with quality estimation. *Machine Translation*, 27(3–4):239–256. DOI: 10.1007/s10590-013-9144-6. 49

Eleftherios Avramidis. 2016. Qualitative: Python tool for MT quality estimation supporting server mode and hybrid MT. *The Prague Bulletin of Mathematical Linguistics*, 106:147–158. DOI: 10.1515/pralin-2016-0014. 118

Eleftherios Avramidis. 2017. QE::GUI—A graphical user interface for quality estimation. *The Prague Bulletin of Mathematical Linguistics*, 109:51–60. DOI: 10.1515/pralin-2017-0038. 118

Eleftherios Avramidis and Maja Popovic. 2013. Selecting feature sets for comparative and time-oriented quality estimation of machine translation output. In *Proc. of the 8th Workshop on Statistical Machine Translation*, pages 329–336. 57

Nguyen Bach, Fei Huang, and Yaser Al-Onaizan. 2011. Goodness: A method for measuring machine translation confidence. In *Proc. of the 49th Annual Meeting of the Association for Computational Linguistics: Human Language Technologies*, pages 211–219. 2, 7

Daniel Beck, Trevor Cohn, Christian Hardmeier, and Lucia Specia. 2015. Learning structural kernels for natural language processing. *Transactions of the Association for Computational Linguistics*, 3:461–473. 57

Daniel Beck, Kashif Shah, Trevor Cohn, and Lucia Specia. 2013a. SHEF-Lite: When less is more for translation quality estimation. In *Proc. of the 8th Workshop on Statistical Machine Translation*, pages 337–342. 57

Daniel Beck, Lucia Specia, and Trevor Cohn. 2013b. Reducing annotation effort for quality estimation via active learning. In *Proc. of the 51st Annual Meeting of the Association for Computational Linguistics*, pages 543–548. 43

Zachary Bergen and Wayne Ward. 1997. A senone based confidence measure for speech recognition. In *Proc. of the 5th European Conference on Speech Communication and Technology*. 7

James Bergstra and Yoshua Bengio. 2012. Random search for hyper-parameter optimization. *Journal of Machine Learning Research*, 13:281–305. 65, 78

Jan Berka, Martin Černý, and Ondřej Bojar. 2011. Quiz-based evaluation of machine translation. *The Prague Bulletin of Mathematical Linguistics*, 95:77–86. DOI: 10.2478/v10108-011-0006-1. 65

Laurent Besacier, Benjamin Lecouteux, Ngoc-Quang Luong, and Ngoc-Tien Le. 2015. Spoken language translation graphs re-decoding using automatic quality assessment. In *Proc. of the IEEE Automatic Speech Recognition and Understanding Workshop*, pages 267–274. DOI: 10.1109/asru.2015.7404804 29

Ergun Biçici. 2013. Referential translation machines for quality estimation. In *Proc. of the 8th Workshop on Statistical Machine Translation*, pages 343–351. 75, 76

Ergun Biçici. 2015. RTM-DCU: Predicting semantic similarity with referential translation machines. In *Proc. of the 9th International Workshop on Semantic Evaluation*, pages 56–63. 76

Ergun Biçici. 2016. Referential translation machines for predicting translation performance. In *Proc. of the 1st Conference on Machine Translation*, pages 777–781. DOI: 10.18653/v1/W16-2382. 74, 78

Ergun Biçici, Declan Groves, and Josef van Genabith. 2013. Predicting sentence translation quality using extrinsic and language independent features. *Machine Translation*, 27:171–192. DOI: 10.1007/s10590-013-9138-4 78

Ergun Biçici, Qun Liu, and Andy Way. 2014. Parallel FDA5 for fast deployment of accurate statistical machine translation systems. In *Proc. of the 9th Workshop on Statistical Machine Translation*, pages 59–65. 76

Ergun Biçici, Qun Liu, and Andy Way. 2015. Referential translation machines for predicting translation quality and related statistics. In *Proc. of the 10th Workshop on Statistical Machine Translation*, pages 304–308. 74, 75

Ergun Biçici and Andy Way. 2014. Referential translation machines for predicting translation quality. In *Proc. of the 9th Workshop on Statistical Machine Translation*, pages 313–321. 57, 75

Frédéric Blain, Varvara Logacheva, and Lucia Specia. 2016. Phrase level segmentation and labelling of machine translation errors. In *Proc. of the 10th Language Resources and Evaluation Conference*, pages 2240–2245. 4

Daniel Blanchard, Joel Tetreault, Derrick Higgins, Aoife Cahill, and Martin Chodorow. 2013. TOEFL11: A corpus of non-native english. *Technical Report*, Educational Testing Service. DOI: 10.1002/j.2333-8504.2013.tb02331.x 106

John Blatz, Erin Fitzgerald, George Foster, Simona Gandrabur, Cyril Goutte, Alex Kulesza, Alberto Sanchis, and Nicola Ueffing. 2003. Confidence estimation for machine translation. *Technical Report*, Johns Hopkins University, Baltimore. 44, 45, 48, 58, 60

John Blatz, Erin Fitzgerald, George Foster, Simona Gandrabur, Cyril Goutte, Alex Kulesza, Alberto Sanchis, and Nicola Ueffing. 2004. Confidence estimation for machine translation. In *Proc. of the 20th International Conference on Computational Linguistics*, pages 315–321. DOI: 10.3115/1220355.1220401 7, 44, 45, 48, 56

Ondrej Bojar, Christian Buck, Chris Callison-Burch, Christian Federmann, Barry Haddow, Philipp Koehn, Christof Monz, Matt Post, Radu Soricut, and Lucia Specia. 2013. Findings of the 2013 workshop on statistical machine translation. In *Proc. of the 8th Workshop on Statistical Machine Translation*, pages 1–44. 3, 7, 13, 45, 49, 50, 51, 115

Ondrej Bojar, Christian Buck, Christian Federmann, Barry Haddow, Philipp Koehn, Johannes Leveling, Christof Monz, Pavel Pecina, Matt Post, Herve Saint-Amand, Radu Soricut, Lucia Specia, and Aleš Tamchyna. 2014. Findings of the 2014 workshop on statistical machine translation. In *Proc. of the 9th Workshop on Statistical Machine Translation*, pages 12–58. DOI: 10.3115/v1/w14-3302 3, 7, 13, 29, 50, 51, 115

Ondřej Bojar, Rajen Chatterjee, Christian Federmann, Yvette Graham, Barry Haddow, Shu-jian Huang, Matthias Huck, Philipp Koehn, Qun Liu, Varvara Logacheva, Christof Monz, Matteo Negri, Matt Post, Raphael Rubino, Lucia Specia, and Marco Turchi. 2017. Findings of the 2017 conference on MT. In *Proc. of the 2nd Conference on Machine Translation*, pages 169–214. 3, 7, 13, 27, 29, 31, 46, 51, 60, 115

Ondřej Bojar, Rajen Chatterjee, Christian Federmann, Yvette Graham, Barry Haddow, Matthias Huck, Antonio Jimeno Yepes, Philipp Koehn, Varvara Logacheva, Christof Monz,

Matteo Negri, Aurelie Neveol, Mariana Neves, Martin Popel, Matt Post, Raphael Rubino, Carolina Scarton, Lucia Specia, Marco Turchi, Karin Verspoor, and Marcos Zampieri. 2016. Findings of the 2016 conference on MT. In *Proc. of the 1st Conference on Machine Translation*, pages 131–198. 3, 7, 13, 27, 29, 46, 51, 63, 69, 115

Ondřej Bojar, Rajen Chatterjee, Christian Federmann, Barry Haddow, Matthias Huck, Chris Hokamp, Philipp Koehn, Varvara Logacheva, Christof Monz, Matteo Negri, Matt Post, Carolina Scarton, Lucia Specia, and Marco Turchi. 2015. Findings of the 2015 workshop on statistical machine translation. In *Proc. of the 10th Workshop on Statistical Machine Translation*, pages 1–46. DOI: 10.18653/v1/w15-3001 3, 7, 13, 46, 51, 64, 115

Christian Buck. 2012. Black box features for the WMT 2012 quality estimation shared task. In *Proc. of the 7th Workshop on Statistical Machine Translation*, pages 91–95. 56

Jill Burstein, Slava Andreyev, and Chi Lu. 2006. Automated essay scoring. U.S. Patent 7,088,949. 82

Jill Burstein, Joel Tetreault, and Slava Andreyev. 2010. Using entity-based features to model coherence in student essays. In *Proc. of the 11th Annual Conference of the North American Chapter of the Association for Computational Linguistics: Human Language Technologies*, pages 681–684. 53

Jill Burstein, Joel Tetreault, and Nitin Madnani. 2013. The E-rater automated essay scoring system. In Mark D. Shermis and Jill Burstein, Eds., *Handbook of Automated Essay Evaluation: Current Applications and New Directions*, pages 55–67, Routledge, NY. DOI: 10.4324/9780203122761.ch4 82

Chris Callison-Burch, Philipp Koehn, Christof Monz, Matt Post, Radu Soricut, and Lucia Specia. 2012. Findings of the 2012 workshop on statistical machine translation. In *Proc. of the 7th Workshop on Statistical Machine Translation*, pages 10–51. 3, 46, 50, 58, 115

José Guilherme Camargo de Souza. 2016. Adaptive quality estimation for machine translation and automatic speech recognition. Ph.D. thesis, Department of Information Engineering and Computer Science, Università Degli Studi di Trento, Trento, Italy. 58

José Guilherme Camargo de Souza, Christian Buck, Marco Turchi, and Matteo Negri. 2013. FBK-UEdin participation to the WMT13 quality estimation shared task. In *Proc. of the 8th Workshop on Statistical Machine Translation*, pages 352–358. 56

José Guilherme Camargo de Souza, Jesús González-Rubio, Christian Buck, Marco Turchi, and Matteo Negri. 2014. FBK-UPV-UEdin participation in the WMT14 quality estimation shared-task. In *Proc. of the 9th Workshop on Statistical Machine Translation*, pages 322–328. DOI: 10.3115/v1/w14-3340 26, 56

Lin Lawrence Chase. 1997. Word and acoustic confidence annotation for large vocabulary speech recognition. In *Proc. of the 5th European Conference on Speech Communication and Technology*, pages 815–818. 7

Rajen Chatterjee, Matteo Negri, Marco Turchi, Marcello Federico, Lucia Specia, and Frédéric Blain. 2017. Guiding neural machine translation decoding with external knowledge. In *Proc. of the 2nd Conference on Machine Translation*, pages 157–168. DOI: 10.18653/v1/w17-4716 8

Kyunghyun Cho, Bart van Merrienboer, Dzmitry Bahdanau, and Yoshua Bengio. 2014. On the properties of neural machine translation: Encoder–decoder approaches. In *Proc. of the 8th Workshop on Syntax, Semantics and Structure in Statistical Translation*, pages 103–111. DOI: 10.3115/v1/w14-4012 26

Trevor Cohn and Lucia Specia. 2013. Modelling annotator bias with multi-task Gaussian processes: An application to machine translation quality estimation. In *Proc. of the 51st Annual Meeting of the Association for Computational Linguistics*, pages 32–42. 57

Daniel Dahlmeier and Hwee Tou Ng. 2012. Better evaluation for grammatical error correction. In *Proc. of the Conference of the North American Chapter of the Association for Computational Linguistics: Human Language Technologies*, pages 568–572. 104

Adrià de Gispert, Graeme Blackwood, Gonzalo Iglesias, and William Byrne, 2013. N-gram posterior probability confidence measures for statistical machine translation: An empirical study. *Machine Translation*, 27(2):85–114. DOI: 10.1007/s10590-012-9132-2 7

Janez Demšar, Zupan Blaž, Gregor Leban, and Tomaz Curk. 2004. Orange: From experimental machine learning to interactive data mining. In *Proc. of the 8th European Conference on Principles and Practice of Knowledge Discovery in Databases*, pages 537–539. DOI: 10.1007/978-3-540-30116-5_58 118

Michael Denkowski and Alon Lavie. 2011. Meteor 1.3: Automatic metric for reliable optimization and evaluation of machine translation systems. In *Proc. of the 6th Workshop on Statistical Machine Translation*, Association for Computational Linguistics, pages 85–91. 74

Nina Dethlefs, Heriberto Cuayáhuitl, Helen Hastie, Verena Rieser, and Oliver Lemon. 2014. Cluster-based prediction of user ratings for stylistic surface realisation. In *Proc. of the 14th Conference of the European Chapter of the Association for Computational Linguistics*, pages 702–711. DOI: 10.3115/v1/e14-1074 109

Robert L. Donaway, Kevin W. Drummey, and Laura A. Mather. 2000. A comparison of rankings produced by summarization evaluation measures. In *Proc. of the Workshop on Automatic Summarization*, pages 69–78. DOI: 10.3115/1567564.1567572. 98

Fei Dong and Yue Zhang. 2016. Automatic features for essay scoring—an empirical study. In *Proc. of the Conference on Empirical Methods in Natural Language Processing*, pages 1072–1077. 82

Ondřej Dušek and Filip Jurčíček. 2015. Training a natural language generator from unaligned data. In *Proc. of the 53rd Annual Meeting of the Association for Computational Linguistics and the 7th International Joint Conference on Natural Language Processing*, pages 451–461. DOI: 10.3115/v1/P15-1044. 109

Ondřej Dušek, Jekaterina Novikova, and Verena Rieser. 2017. Referenceless quality estimation for natural language generations. In *Proc. of the 1st Workshop on Learning to Generate Natural Language*. 109, 110

Miquel Esplà-Gomis, Felipe Sánchez-Martínez, and Mikel Forcada, 2015. UAlacant word-level machine translation quality estimation system at WMT. In *Proc. of the 10th Workshop on Statistical Machine Translation*, pages 309–315. DOI: 10.18653/v1/w15-3036 22

Miquel Esplà-Gomis, Felipe Sánchez-Martínez, and Mikel Forcada, 2016. UAlacant word-level and phrase-level machine translation quality estimation systems at WMT. In *Proc. of the 1st Conference on Machine Translation*, pages 782–786. DOI: 10.18653/v1/w16-2383 22

Mariano Felice and Ted Briscoe. 2015. Towards a standard evaluation method for grammatical error detection and correction. In *Proc. of the Conference of the North American Chapter of the Association for Computational Linguistics: Human Language Technologies*, pages 578–587. DOI: 10.3115/v1/N15-1060. 104

Mariano Felice and Lucia Specia. 2012. Linguistic features for quality estimation. In *Proc. of the 7th Workshop on Statistical Machine Translation*, pages 96–103. 56

Pablo Fetter, Frédéric Dandurand, and Peter Regel-Brietzmann. 1996. Word graph rescoring using confidence measures. In *Proc. of the 4th International Conference on Spoken Language Processing*, pages 10–13. DOI: 10.1109/icslp.1996.606917 6, 8, 9

Lluís Formiga, Meritxell Gonzàlez, Alberto Barrón-Cedeño, José A. R. Fonollosa, and Lluis Marquez. 2013. The TALP-UPC approach to system selection: Asiya features and pairwise classification using random forests. In *Proc. of the 8th Workshop on Statistical Machine Translation*, pages 359–364. 57

Michael Gamon, Anthony Aue, and Martine Smets. 2005. Sentence-level MT evaluation without reference translations: Beyond language modeling. In *Proc. of the 10th Annual Conference of the European Association for Machine Translation*, pages 103–111. 48

Simona Gandrabur and George Foster. 2003. Confidence estimation for translation prediction. In *Proc. of the Conference of the North American Chapter of the Association for Computational*

Linguistics: Human Language Technologies, pages 95–102. DOI: 10.3115/1119176.1119189. 7

Albert Gatt and Emiel Krahmer. 2018. Survey of the state of the art in natural language generation: Core tasks, applications and evaluation. *Journal of Artificial Intelligence Research*, 61:65–170. DOI: 10.1613/jair.5477. 108, 109

Debanjan Ghosh, Aquila Khanam, Yubo Han, and Smaranda Muresan. 2016. Coarse-grained argumentation features for scoring persuasive essays. In *Proc. of the 54th Annual Meeting of the Association for Computational Linguistics*, pages 549–554. DOI: 10.18653/v1/p16-2089 82

George Giannakopoulos. 2013. Multi-document multilingual summarization and evaluation tracks in ACL 2013 MultiLing Workshop. In *Proc. of the Workshop on Multilingual Multi-document Summarization*, pages 20–28. 98

George Giannakopoulos, John M. Conroy, Jeff Kubina, Peter A. Rankel, Elena Lloret, Josef Steinberger, Marina Litvak, and Benoit Favre. 2017. MultiLing 2017 overview. In *Proc. of the Workshop on Multilingual Multi-document Summarization*, pages 1–6. DOI: 10.18653/v1/w17-1001 98

George Giannakopoulos, Jeff Kubina, John M. Conroy, Josef Steinberger, Benoit Favre, Mijail Kabadjov, Udo Kruschwitz, and Massimo Poesio. 2015. MultiLing: Multilingual summarization of single and multi-documents, on-line fora, and call-center conversations. In *Proc. of the SIGDIAL Conference*, pages 270–274. DOI: 10.18653/v1/w15-4638 98

Jesús Giménez and Lluís Màrquez. 2010. Asiya: An open toolkit for automatic machine translation (meta-)evaluation. *The Prague Bulletin of Mathematical Linguistics*, (94):77–86. DOI: 10.2478/v10108-010-0022-6. 118

Goran Glavaš and Sanja Štajner. 2013. Event-centered simplification of news stories. In *Proc. of the RANLP Student Research Workshop*, pages 71–78. 86

Goran Glavaš and Sanja Štajner. 2015. Simplifying lexical simplification: Do we need simplified corpora? In *Proc. of the 53rd Annual Meeting of the Association for Computational Linguistics and the 7th International Joint Conference on Natural Language Processing*, pages 63–69. DOI: 10.3115/v1/P15-2011. 82, 84, 86

Dan Goldwasser, Roi Reichart, James Clarke, and Dan Roth. 2011. Confidence driven unsupervised semantic parsing. In *Proc. of the 49th Annual Meeting of the Association for Computational Linguistics: Human Language Technologies*, pages 1486–1495. 7

Ian J. Goodfellow, David Warde-Farley, Mehdi Mirza, Aaron C. Courville, and Yoshua Bengio. 2013. Maxout networks. In *Proc. of the 30th International Conference on Machine Learning*, pages 1319–1327. 33

Arthur C. Graesser, Danielle S. McNamara, Max M. Louwerse, and Zhiqiang Cai. 2004. Coh-metrix: Analysis of text on cohesion and language. *Behavior Research Methods*, 36(2):193–202. DOI: 10.3758/bf03195564 90

Yvette Graham. 2015. Improving evaluation of machine translation quality estimation. In *Proc. of the 53rd Annual Meeting of the Association for Computational Linguistics and the 7th International Joint Conference on Natural Language Processing*, pages 1804–1813. DOI: 10.3115/v1/P15-1174. 58

Christian Hardmeier, Joakim Nivre, and Jörg Tiedemann. 2012. Tree kernels for machine translation quality estimation. In *Proc. of the 7th Workshop on Statistical Machine Translation*, pages 109–113. 56, 57

Yifan He, Yanjun Ma, Josef van Genabith, and Andy Way. 2010. Bridging SMT and TM with translation recommendation. In *Proc. of the 48th Annual Meeting of the Association for Computational Linguistics*, pages 622–630. 2, 46

Michael Heilman, Aoife Cahill, Nitin Madnani, Melissa Lopez, Matthew Mulholland, and Joel Tetreault. 2014. Predicting grammaticality on an ordinal scale. In *Proc. of the 52nd Annual Meeting of the Association for Computational Linguistics*, pages 174–180. DOI: 10.3115/v1/p14-2029 81, 106, 121

Silja Hildebrand and Stephan Vogel. 2013. MT quality estimation: The CMU system for WMT. In *Proc. of the 8th Workshop on Statistical Machine Translation*, pages 373–379. 56

Sepp Hochreiter and Jürgen Schmidhuber. 1997. Long short-term memory. *Neural Computation*, 9(8):1735–1780. DOI: 10.1162/neco.1997.9.8.1735. 26

Chris Hokamp. 2017. Ensembling factored neural machine translation models for automatic post-editing and quality estimation. In *Proc. of the 2nd Conference on Machine Translation*, pages 647–654. 27, 31, 36, 38, 39, 40, 41, 117

Colby Horn, Cathryn Manduca, and David Kauchak. 2014. Learning a lexical simplifier using Wikipedia. In *Proc. of the 52nd Annual Meeting of the Association for Computational Linguistics*, pages 458–463. DOI: 10.3115/v1/P14-2075. 82

Julia Ive, Frédéric Blain, and Lucia Specia. 2018. deepQuest: A framework for neural-based quality estimation. In *Proc. of the 27th International Conference on Computational Linguistics*. 117

Hui Jiang. 2005. Confidence measures for speech recognition: A survey. *Speech Communication*, 45(4):455–470. DOI: 10.1016/j.specom.2004.12.004. 7, 9, 108

Takatoshi Jitsuhiro, Satoshi Takahashi, and Kiyoaki Aikawa. 1998. Rejection of out-of-vocabulary words using phoneme confidence likelihood. In *Proc. of the IEEE International Conference on Acoustics, Speech and Signal Processing*, vol. 1, pages 217–220. DOI: 10.1109/icassp.1998.674406 8

Douglas A. Jones, Edward Gibson, Wade Shen, Neil Granoien, Martha Herzog, Douglas Reynolds, and Clifford Weinstein. 2005a. Measuring translation quality by testing english speakers with a new defense language proficiency test for arabic. In *Proc. of the International Conference on Intelligence Analysis.* 65

Douglas A. Jones, Wade Shen, Neil Granoien, Martha Herzog, and Clifford Weinstein. 2005b. Measuring human readability of machine generated text: Three case studies in speech recognition and machine translation. In *Proc. of the IEEE International Conference on Acoustics, Speech, and Signal Processing*, pages 1009–1012. DOI: 10.1109/icassp.2005.1416477 65

Marcin Junczys-Dowmunt and Roman Grundkiewicz. 2016. Log-linear combinations of monolingual and bilingual neural machine translation models for automatic post-editing. In *Proc. of the 1st Conference on Machine Translation*, pages 751–758. DOI: 10.18653/v1/W16-2378. 39

David Kauchak. 2013. Improving text simplification language modeling using unsimplified text data. In *Proc. of the 51st Annual Meeting of the Association for Computational Linguistics*, pages 1537–1546. 88

Hyun Kim, Hun-Young Jung, Hongseok Kwon, Jong-Hyeok Lee, and Seung-Hoon Na, 2017a. Predictor-estimator: Neural quality estimation based on target word prediction for machine translation. *ACM Transactions on Asian and Low-Resource Language Information Processing*, 17(1):3. DOI: 10.1145/3109480 38

Hyun Kim and Jong-Hyeok Lee. 2016. Recurrent neural network based translation quality estimation. In *Proc. of the 1st Conference on Machine Translation*, pages 787–792. DOI: 10.18653/v1/W16-2384. 26, 57

Hyun Kim, Jong-Hyeok Lee, and Seung-Hoon Na. 2017b. Predictor-estimator using multi-level task learning with stack propagation for neural quality estimation. In *Proc. of the 2nd Conference on Machine Translation*, pages 562–568. 16, 26, 31, 32, 33, 34, 35, 38, 41, 56, 57, 60, 75, 117

J. Peter Kincaid, Robert P. Fishburne Jr., Richard L. Rogers, and Brad S. Chissom. 1975. Derivation of new readability formulas (automated readability index, fog count and flesch reading ease formula) for navy enlisted personnel. *Technical Report*, Naval Technical Training Command, Millington TN Research Branch. DOI: 10.21236/ada006655 90

Ryan Kiros, Yukun Zhu, Ruslan Salakhutdinov, Richard S. Zemel, Antonio Torralba, Raquel Urtasun, and Sanja Fidler. 2015. Skip-thought vectors. In *Proc. of the 28th International Conference on Neural Information Processing Systems*, pages 3294–3302. 116

Philipp Koehn. 2005. Europarl: A parallel corpus for statistical machine translation. In *Proc. of the 10th Machine Translation Summit*, pages 79–86. 32

Maarit Koponen, Wilker Aziz, Luciana Ramos, and Lucia Specia. 2012. Post-editing time as a measure of cognitive effort. In *Proc. of the Workshop on Post-Editing Technology and Practice*, pages 11–20. 50, 120

Anna Kozlova, Mariya Shmatova, and Anton Frolov. 2016. YSDA Participation in the WMT Quality Estimation Shared Task. In *Proc. of the 1st Conference on Machine Translation*, pages 793–799. DOI: 10.18653/v1/w16-2385 56

Hans P. Krings. 2001. *Repairing Texts: Empirical Investigations of Machine Translation Post-editing Process*. The Kent State University Press, Kent, OH. 49

Shankar Kumar, Wolfgang Macherey, Chris Dyer, and Franz Och. 2009. Efficient minimum error rate training and minimum Bayes-risk decoding for translation hypergraphs and lattices. In *Proc. of the 47th Annual Meeting of the Association for Computational Linguistics and the 4th International Joint Conference on Natural Language Processing of the Asian Federation of Natural Language Processing*, pages 163–171. DOI: 10.3115/1687878.1687903 8

John D. Lafferty, Andrew McCallum, and Fernando C. N. Pereira. 2001. Conditional random fields: Probabilistic models for segmenting and labeling sequence data. In *Proc. of the 18th International Conference on Machine Learning*, pages 282–289. 24

Gerasimos Lampouras and Andreas Vlachos. 2016. Imitation learning for language generation from unaligned data. In *Proc. of the 26th International Conference on Computational Linguistics*, pages 1101–1112. 109

Thomas K. Landauer and Susan T. Dumais. 1997. A solution to Plato's problem: The latent semantic analysis theory of acquisition, induction, and representation of knowledge. *Psychological Review*, 104(2):211–240. 71

David Langlois, Sylvain Raybaud, and Kamel Smaïli. 2012. LORIA system for the WMT quality estimation shared task. In *Proc. of the 7th Workshop on Statistical Machine Translation*, pages 114–119. DOI: 10.18653/v1/w15-3038 56

Thomas Lavergne, Olivier Cappé, and François Yvon. 2010. Practical very large scale CRFs. In *Proc. of the 48th Annual Meeting of the Association for Computational Linguistics*, pages 504–513. 118

Chin-Yew Lin. 2004. ROUGE: A package for automatic evaluation of summaries. In *Proc. of the Workshop on Text Summarization Branches Out*, pages 74–81. 98

Chin-Yew Lin and Eduard Hovy. 2003. Automatic evaluation of summaries using N-gram co-occurrence statistics. In *Proc. of the Conference of the North American Chapter of the Association for Computational Linguistics: Human Language Technologies*, pages 71–78. DOI: 10.3115/1073445.1073465. 98

Eduardo Lleida and Richard C. Rose. 2000. Utterance verification in continuous speech recognition: Decoding and training procedures. *IEEE Transactions on Speech and Audio Processing*, 8(2):126–139. DOI: 10.1109/89.824697. 8

Varvara Logacheva, Frédéric Blain, and Lucia Specia. 2016a. USFD's phrase-level quality estimation systems. In *Proc. of the 1st Conference on Machine Translation*, pages 800–805. DOI: 10.18653/v1/w16-2386 19, 25

Varvara Logacheva, Chris Hokamp, and Lucia Specia. 2016b. MARMOT: A toolkit for translation quality estimation at the word level. In *Proc. of the 10th Language Resources and Evaluation Conference*, pages 3671–3674. 118

Varvara Logacheva, Michal Lukasik, and Lucia Specia. 2016c. Metrics for evaluation of word-level machine translation quality estimation. In *Proc. of the 54th Annual Meeting of the Association for Computational Linguistics*, pages 585–590. DOI: 10.18653/v1/p16-2095 29

Varvara Logacheva and Lucia Specia. 2015. The role of artificially generated negative data for quality estimation of machine translation. In *Proc. of the 18th Annual Conference of the European Association for Machine Translation*. 117

Arle Lommel, Hans Uszkoreit, and Aljoscha Burchardt. 2014. Multidimensional quality metrics (MQM): A framework for declaring and describing translation quality metrics. *Tradumàtica*, (12):455–463. DOI: 10.5565/rev/tradumatica.77 10

Annie Louis and Ani Nenkova. 2013. Automatically assessing machine summary content without a gold standard. *Computational Linguistics*, 39(2):267–300. DOI: 10.1162/COLI_a_00123. 98, 99, 102, 104

Ngoc Quang Luong, Laurent Besacier, and Benjamin Lecouteux. 2014a. LIG system for word level QE task at WMT. In *Proc. of the 9th Workshop on Statistical Machine Translation*, pages 335–341. DOI: 10.3115/v1/w14-3342 25

Ngoc Quang Luong, Laurent Besacier, and Benjamin Lecouteux. 2014b. Word confidence estimation for SMT N-best list re-ranking. In *Proc. of the Workshop on Humans and Computer-assisted Translation*, pages 1–9. DOI: 10.3115/v1/w14-0301 8

Ngoc Quang Luong, Benjamin Lecouteux, and Laurent Besacier. 2013. LIG system for WMT QE task: Investigating the usefulness of features in word confidence estimation for MT. In *Proc. of the 8th Workshop on Statistical Machine Translation*, pages 386–391. DOI: 10.13140/RG.2.1.4757.7764. 25

François Mairesse, Milica Gašić, Filip Jurčíček, Simon Keizer, Blaise Thomson, Kai Yu, and Steve Young. 2010. Phrase-based statistical language generation using graphical models and active learning. In *Proc. of the 48th Annual Meeting of the Association for Computational Linguistics*, pages 1552–1561. 109

François Mairesse and Marilyn Walker. 2011. Controlling user perceptions of linguistic style: Trainable generation of personality traits. *Computational Linguistics*, 37:455–488. DOI: 10.1162/COLI_a_00063. 109

Alvin F. Martin, George Doddington, Terri Kamm, Mark Ordowski, and Mark Przybocki. 1997. The DET curve in assessment of detection task performance. *Technical Report*, National Institute of Standards and Technology, Gaithersburg MD. 30

Alvin F. Martin and Mark A. Przybocki. 2003. NIST language recognition evaluation. In *Proc. of the 18th European Conference on Speech Communication and Technology*, pages 1341–1344. 44

André F. T. Martins, Ramón Astudillo, Chris Hokamp, and Fabio N. Kepler. 2016. Unbabel's participation in the WMT word-level translation quality estimation shared task. In *Proc. of the 1st Conference on Machine Translation*, pages 806–811. DOI: 10.18653/v1/w16-2387 15, 26

André F. T. Martins, Marcin Junczys-Dowmunt, Fabio N. Kepler, Ramón Astudillo, Chris Hokamp, and Roman Grundkiewicz. 2017a. Pushing the limits of translation quality estimation. *Transactions of the Association for Computational Linguistics*, 5:205–218. 16, 27, 31, 35, 36, 37, 38, 57, 60, 117

André F. T. Martins, Fabio N. Kepler, and José Monteiro. 2017b. Unbabel's participation in the WMT translation quality estimation shared task. In *Proc. of the 2nd Conference on Machine Translation*, pages 569–574. DOI: 10.18653/v1/w17-4764 36, 38, 56, 57

Sandeep Mathias and Pushpak Bhattacharyya. 2016. Using machine translation evaluation techniques to evaluate text simplification systems. In *Proc. of the 1st Quality Assessment for Text Simplification Workshop*, pages 38–41. 90

G. Harry McLaughlin. 1969. SMOG grading—a new readability formula. *Journal of Reading*, 12(8):639–646. 90

Detmar Meurers, Ramon Ziai, Niels Ott, and Janina Kopp. 2011. Evaluating answers to reading comprehension questions in context: Results for German and the role of information structure. In *Proc. of the Workshop on Textual Entailment*, pages 1–9. 65

Tomas Mikolov, Ilya Sutskever, Kai Chen, Greg S. Corrado, and Jeff Dean. 2013a. Distributed representations of words and phrases and their compositionality. In *Proc. of the 26th Advances in Neural Information Processing Systems*, pages 3111–3119. 16

Tomas Mikolov, Wen-tau Yih, and Geoffrey Zweig. 2013b. Linguistic regularities in continuous space word representations. In *Proc. of the Conference of the North American Chapter of the Association for Computational Linguistics: Human Language Technologies*, pages 746–751. 73

George A. Miller. 1995. WordNet: A lexical database for English. *Communications of the ACM*, 38(11):39–41. DOI: 10.1145/219717.219748. 16

Courtney Napoles, Keisuke Sakaguchi, Matt Post, and Joel Tetreault. 2015. Ground truth for grammatical error correction metrics. In *Proc. of the 53rd Annual Meeting of the Association for Computational Linguistics and the 7th International Joint Conference on Natural Language Processing*, pages 588–593. DOI: 10.3115/v1/p15-2097 104

Courtney Napoles, Keisuke Sakaguchi, and Joel Tetreault. 2016. There's no comparison: Reference-less evaluation metrics in grammatical error correction. In *Proc. of the Conference on Empirical Methods on Natural Language Processing*, pages 2109–2115. 105, 106, 107, 108

Courtney Napoles, Keisuke Sakaguchi, and Joel Tetreault. 2017. JFLEG: A fluency corpus and benchmark for grammatical error correction. In *Proc. of the 15th Conference of the European Chapter of the Association for Computational Linguistics*, pages 229–234. 107, 121

Roberto Navigli and Simone Paolo Ponzetto. 2012. BabelNet: The automatic construction, evaluation and application of a wide-coverage multilingual semantic network. *Artificial Intelligence*, 193:217–250. DOI: 10.1016/j.artint.2012.07.001. 16

Matteo Negri, Marco Turchi, José G. C. de Souza, and Daniele Falavigna. 2014. Quality estimation for automatic speech recognition. In *Proc. of the 25th International Conference on Computational Linguistics*, pages 1813–1823. 8, 108

Ani Nenkova and Kathleen McKeown. 2011. Automatic summarization. *Foundations and Trends in Information Retrieval*, 5(2–3):103–233. DOI: 10.1561/1500000015. 97

Ani Nenkova, Rebecca Passonneau, and Kathleen McKeown. 2007. The pyramid method: Incorporating human content selection variation in summarization evaluation. *ACM Transactions on Speech and Language Processing*, 4(2):4. DOI: 10.1145/1233912.1233913. 98

Ani Nenkova and Lucy Vanderwende. 2005. The impact of frequency on summarization. *Technical Report MSR-TR-2005-101*, Microsoft. 102

Chalapathy V. Neti, Salim Roukos, and Ellen Eide. 1997. Word-based confidence measures as a guide for stack search in speech recognition. In *Proc. of the IEEE International Conference on Acoustics, Speech, and Signal Processing*, pages 883–886. DOI: 10.1109/ICASSP.1997.596077. 8

Newsela. 2016. Newsela article corpus. `https://newsela.com/data` 88

Hwee Tou Ng, Siew Mei Wu, Ted Briscoe, Christian Hadiwinoto, Raymond Hendy Susanto, and Christopher Bryant. 2014. The CoNLL shared task on grammatical error correction. In *Proc. of the 8th Conference on Computational Natural Language Learning: Shared Task*, pages 1–14. DOI: 10.3115/v1/w14-1701 81, 104, 106

Hwee Tou Ng, Siew Mei Wu, Yuanbin Wu, Christian Hadiwinoto, and Joel Tetreault. 2013. The CoNLL shared task on grammatical error correction. In *Proc. of the 7th Conference on Computational Natural Language Learning: Shared Task*, pages 1–12. 81, 104

Raymond W. M. Ng, Kashif Shah, Wilker Aziz, Lucia Specia, and Thomas Hain, 2015a. Quality estimation for ASR k-best list rescoring in spoken language translation. In *Proc. of the IEEE International Conference on Acoustics, Speech, and Signal Processing*, pages 5226–5230. DOI: 10.1109/icassp.2015.7178968 45

Raymond W. M. Ng, Kashif Shah, Lucia Specia, and Thomas Hain, 2015b. A study on the stability and effectiveness of features in quality estimation for spoken language translation. In *Proc. of the Conference of the International Speech Communication Association*, pages 2257–2261. 45

Raymond W. M. Ng, Kashif Shah, Lucia Specia, and Thomas Hain. 2016. Groupwise learning for ASR k-best list reranking in spoken language translation. In *Proc. of the IEEE International Conference on Acoustics, Speech, and Signal Processing*, pages 6120–6124. DOI: 10.1109/ICASSP.2016.7472853. 45

Sergiu Nisioi and Fabrice Nauze. 2016. An ensemble method for quality assessment of text simplification. In *Proc. of the 1st Quality Assessment for Text Simplification Workshop*, pages 47–52. 90, 91, 93, 96

Sergiu Nisioi, Sanja Štajner, Simone Paolo Ponzetto, and Liviu P. Dinu. 2017. Exploring neural text simplification models. In *Proc. of the 55th Annual Meeting of the Association for Computational Linguistics*, pages 85–91. DOI: 10.18653/v1/p17-2014 82

Franz Josef Och, Daniel Gildea, Sanjeev Khudanpur, Anoop Sarkar, Kenji Yamada, Alex Fraser, Shankar Kumar, Libin Shen, David Smith, Katherine Eng, Viren Jain, Zhen Jin, and Dragomir Radev. 2004. A smorgasbord of features for statistical machine translation. In *Proc. of the Conference of the North American Chapter of the Association for Computational Linguistics: Human Language Technologies*, pages 161–168. 45

Naoaki Okazaki. 2007. CRFsuite: A fast implementation of conditional random fields. `http://www.chokkan.org/software/crfsuite/` 118

Niels Ott, Ramon Ziai, and Detmar Meurers. 2012. Creation and analysis of a reading comprehension exercise corpus: Towards evaluating meaning in context. In T. Schmidt and K. Worner, Eds., *Multilingual Corpora and Multilingual Corpus Analysis*, pages 47–69. DOI: 10.1075/hsm.14.05ott. 65

Gustavo Paetzold and Lucia Specia. 2016a. SimpleNets: Quality estimation with resource-light neural networks. In *Proc. of the 1st Conference on Machine Translation*, pages 812–818. DOI: 10.18653/v1/W16-2388. 56, 57

Gustavo Paetzold and Lucia Specia. 2017. Lexical simplification with neural ranking. In *Proc. of the 15th Conference of the European Chapter of the Association for Computational Linguistics*, pages 34–40. DOI: 10.18653/v1/E17-2006. 82

Gustavo H. Paetzold and Lucia Specia. 2013. Text simplification as tree transduction. In *Proc. of the 9th Brazilian Symposium in Information and Human Language Technology*, pages 116–125. 84

Gustavo Henrique Paetzold and Lucia Specia. 2016b. SimpleNets: Evaluating simplifiers with resource-light neural networks. In *Proc. of the 1st Quality Assessment for Text Simplification Workshop*, pages 42–46. DOI: 10.18653/v1/W16-2388. 91, 92

Gustavo Henrique Paetzold, Lucia Specia, and Yves Savourel. 2015. Okapi+QuEst: Translation quality estimation within Okapi. In *Proc. of the 18th Annual Conference of the European Association for Machine Translation*, page 222. 118

Daniel Paiva and Roger Evans. 2005. Empirically-based control of natural language generation. In *Proc. of the 43rd Annual Meeting of the Association for Computational Linguistics*, pages 58–65. 109

Kishore Papineni, Salim Roukos, Todd Ward, and Wei-Jing Zhu. 2002. BLEU: A method for automatic evaluation of machine translation. In *Proc. of the 40th Annual Meeting of the Association for Computational Linguistics*, pages 311–318. DOI: 10.3115/1073083.1073135. 45

Robert Parker, David Graff, Junbo Kong, Ke Chen, and Kazuaki Maeda. 2011. *English Gigaword* 5th ed., LDC2011T07. Philadelphia: Linguistic Data Consortium. 105

Carla Parra Escartín, Hannah Béchara, and Constantin Orasan. 2017. Questing for quality estimation—a user study. *The Prague Bulletin of Mathematical Linguistics*, 108:343–354. DOI: 10.1515/pralin-2017-0032 47, 48, 51

Fabian Pedregosa, Gaël Varoquaux, Alexandre Gramfort, Vincent Michel, Bertrand Thirion, Olivier Grisel, Mathieu Blondel, Peter Prettenhofer, Ron Weiss, Vincent Dubourg, Jake Vanderplas, Alexandre Passos, David Cournapeau, Matthieu Brucher, Matthieu Perrot, and Édouard Duchesnay. 2011. Scikit-learn: Machine learning in Python. *Journal of Machine Learning Research*, 12:2825–2830. 118

Isaac Persing and Vincent Ng. 2013. Modeling thesis clarity in student essays. In *Proc. of the 51st Annual Meeting of the Association for Computational Linguistics*, pages 260–269. 82

Isaac Persing and Vincent Ng. 2014. Modeling prompt adherence in student essays. In *Proc. of the 52nd Annual Meeting of the Association for Computational Linguistics*, pages 1534–1543. DOI: 10.3115/v1/P14-1144. 82

Isaac Persing and Vincent Ng. 2016a. End-to-end argumentation mining in student essays. In *Proc. of the Conference of the North American Chapter of the Association for Computational Linguistics: Human Language Technologies*, pages 1384–1394. DOI: 10.18653/v1/N16-1164. 82

Isaac Persing and Vincent Ng. 2016b. Modeling stance in student essays. In *Proc. of the 54th Annual Meeting of the Association for Computational Linguistics*, pages 2174–2184. DOI: 10.18653/v1/P16-1205. 82

Emily Pitler and Ani Nenkova. 2009. Using syntax to disambiguate explicit discourse connectives in text. In *Proc. of the 47th Annual Meeting of the ACL and the 4th International Joint Conference on Natural Language Processing of the AFNLP*, pages 13–16. DOI: 10.3115/1667583.1667589. 72

Mirko Plitt and François Masselot. 2010. A productivity test of statistical machine translation post-editing in a typical localisation context. *The Prague Bulletin of Mathematical Linguistics*, 93:7–16. DOI: 10.2478/v10108-010-0010-x. 46

Maja Popović and Sanja Štajner. 2016. Machine translation evaluation metrics for quality assessment of automatically simplified sentences. In *Proc. of the 1st Quality Assessment for Text Simplification Workshop*, pages 32–37. 89

Marion Potet, Emmanuelle Esperança-Rodier, Laurent Besacier, and Hervé Blanchon. 2012. Collection of a large database of French-English SMT output corrections. In *Proc. of the 8th Language Resources and Evaluation Conference*, pages 4043–4048. 120

C. B. Quirk. 2004. Training a sentence-level machine translation confidence measure. In *Proc. of the 4th Language Resources and Evaluation Conference*, pages 825–828. 44, 48, 56, 58, 60

Peter A. Rankel, John M. Conroy, and Judith D. Schlesinger. 2012. Better metrics to automatically predict the quality of a text summary. *Algorithms*, 5:398–420. DOI: 10.3390/a5040398. 99

Sylvain Raybaud, David Langlois, and Kamel Smaïli. 2011. "This sentence is wrong." Detecting errors in machine-translated sentences. *Machine Translation*, 25(1):1–34. DOI: 10.1007/s10590-011-9094-9 14

Roi Reichart and Ari Rappoport. 2009. Automatic selection of high quality parses created by a fully unsupervised parser. In *Proc. of the 13th Conference on Computational Natural Language Learning*, pages 156–164. DOI: 10.3115/1596374.1596400. 7

Ehud Reiter and Robert Dale. 2000. *Building Natural Language Generation Systems*. Cambridge University Press, Cambridge, UK. 108

Matthew Richardson, Christopher J. C. Burges, and Erin Renshaw. 2013. MCTest: A challenge dataset for the open-domain machine comprehension of text. In *Proc. of the Conference on Empirical Methods on Natural Language Processing*, pages 193–203. 78

Matīss Rikters and Mark Fishel. 2017. Confidence through attention. In *Proc. of the 16th Machine Translation Summit*, pages 305–317. 8

Raphael Rubino, Joachim Wagner, Jennifer Foster, Johann Roturier, Rasoul Samad Zadeh Kaljahi, and Fred Hollowood. 2013. DCU-Symantec at the WMT quality estimation shared task. In *Proc. of the 8th Workshop on Statistical Machine Translation*, pages 392–397. 22

Horacio Saggion, Juan-Manuel Torres-Moreno, Iria da Cunha, and Eric SanJuan, 2010. Multilingual summarization evaluation without human models. In *Proc. of the 23rd International Conference on Computational Linguistics*, pages 1059–1067, Beijing, China. 98

Keisuke Sakaguchi, Courtney Napoles, Matt Post, and Joel Tetreault. 2016. Reassessing the goals of grammatical error correction: Fluency instead of grammaticality. *Transactions of the Association for Computational Linguistics*, 4:169–182. 81, 107

Carolina Scarton. 2015. Discourse and document-level information for evaluating language output tasks. In *Proc. of the NAACL-HLT Student Research Workshop*, pages 118–125. DOI: 10.3115/v1/N15-2016. 61

Carolina Scarton. 2017. Document-level machine translation quality estimation. Ph.D. thesis, Department of Computer Science, University of Sheffield, Sheffield, UK. 3, 61, 63, 64, 65, 69, 71, 72, 73, 74, 75, 76, 78, 79

Carolina Scarton, Daniel Beck, Kashif Shah, Karin Sim Smith, and Lucia Specia, 2016. Word embeddings and discourse information for machine translation quality estimation. In *Proc. of the 1st Conference on Machine Translation*, pages 831–837. DOI: 10.18653/v1/w16-2391 73, 74, 77, 78

Carolina Scarton and Lucia Specia. 2014a. Document-level translation quality estimation: Exploring discourse and pseudo-references. In *Proc. of the 17th Annual Conference of the European Association for Machine Translation*, pages 101–108. 3, 61, 63, 64, 71, 74

Carolina Scarton and Lucia Specia. 2014b. Exploring consensus in machine translation for quality estimation. In *Proc. of the 9th Workshop on Statistical Machine Translation*, pages 342–347. DOI: 10.3115/v1/W14-3343. 74

Carolina Scarton and Lucia Specia. 2015. A quantitative analysis of discourse phenomena in machine translation. *Discours—Revue de Linguistique, Psycholinguistique et Informatique*, (16). DOI: 10.4000/discours.9047. 72

Carolina Scarton and Lucia Specia. 2016. A reading comprehension corpus for machine translation evaluation. In *Proc. of the 10th Language Resources and Evaluation Conference*, pages 3652–3658. 63, 64, 65, 66, 67, 120

Carolina Scarton, Liling Tan, and Lucia Specia. 2015a. USHEF and USAAR-USHEF participation in the WMT QE shared task. In *Proc. of the 10th Workshop on Statistical Machine Translation*, pages 336–341. DOI: 10.18653/v1/w15-3040 74

Carolina Scarton, Marcos Zampieri, Mihaela Vela, Josef van Genabith, and Lucia Specia. 2015b. Searching for context: A study on document-level labels for translation quality estimation. In *Proc. of the 18th Annual Conference of the European Association for Machine Translation*, pages 121–128. 61, 63, 64, 66, 68, 76

Jürgen Schürmann. 1996. *Pattern Classification: A Unified View of Statistical and Neural Approaches*. Wiley Online Library. DOI: 10.1080/00401706.1997.10485447. 6

Christophe Servan, Ngoc-Tien Le, Ngoc Quang Luong, Benjamin Lecouteux, and Laurent Besacier. 2015. An open source toolkit for word-level confidence estimation in machine translation. In *Proc. of the 12th International Workshop on Spoken Language Translation*. 118

Kashif Shah, Fethi Bougares, Loïc Barrault, and Lucia Specia. 2016. SHEF-LIUM-NN: Sentence level quality estimation with neural network features. In *Proc. of the 1st Conference on Machine Translation*, pages 838–842. DOI: 10.18653/v1/w16-2392 56

Kashif Shah, Trevor Cohn, and Lucia Specia. 2015a. A Bayesian non-linear method for feature selection in machine translation quality estimation. *Machine Translation*, 21(2):101–125. DOI: 10.1007/s10590-014-9164-x 56

Kashif Shah, Varvara Logacheva, Gustavo Paetzold, Frédéric Blain, Daniel Beck, Fethi Bougares, and Lucia Specia. 2015b. SHEF-NN: Translation quality estimation with neural networks. In *Proc. of the 10th Workshop on Statistical Machine Translation*, pages 342–347. DOI: 10.18653/v1/w15-3041 16, 56

Kashif Shah and Lucia Specia. 2014. Quality estimation for translation selection. In *Proc. of the 11th Annual Conference of the European Association for Machine Translation*, pages 109–116. 2, 46, 57, 60

Liugang Shang, Dongfeng Cai, and Duo Ji. 2015. Strategy-based technology for estimating MT quality. In *Proc. of the 10th Workshop on Statistical Machine Translation*, pages 348–352. DOI: 10.18653/v1/W15-3042. 25

Advaith Siddharthan and Angrosh Mandya. 2014. Hybrid text simplification using synchronous dependency grammars with hand-written and automatically harvested rules. In *Proc. of the 14th Conference of the European Chapter of the Association for Computational Linguistics*, pages 722–731. DOI: 10.3115/v1/E14-1076. 82

Abhishek Singh and Wei Jin. 2016. Ranking summaries for informativeness and coherence without reference summaries. In *Proc. of the 29th International Florida Artificial Intelligence Research Society Conference*, pages 104–109. 102, 104

Anil Kumar Singh, Guillaume Wisniewski, and François Yvon. 2013. LIMSI submission for the WMT quality estimation task: An experiment with N-gram posteriors. In *Proc. of the 8th Workshop on Statistical Machine Translation*, pages 398–404. 22

Matthew Snover, Bonnie Dorr, Richard Schwartz, Linnea Micciulla, and John Makhoul. 2006. A study of translation edit rate with targeted human annotation. In *Proc. of the 7th Biennial Conference of the Association for Machine Translation in the Americas*, pages 223–231. 46

Matthew Snover, Nitin Madnani, Bonnie Dorr, and Richard Schwartz. 2010. TER-Plus: Paraphrase, semantic, and alignment enhancements to translation edit rate. *Machine Translation (Special Issue on Automated Metrics for MT Evaluation)*, 23(2–3):117–127. DOI: 10.1007/s10590-009-9062-9 46

Radu Soricut, Nguyen Bach, and Ziyuan Wang. 2012. The SDL language weaver systems in the WMT12 quality estimation shared task. In *Proc. of the 7th Workshop on Statistical Machine Translation*, pages 145–151. 56

Radu Soricut and Abdessamad Echihabi. 2010. TrustRank: Inducing trust in automatic translations via ranking. In *Proc. of the 48th Annual Meeting of the Association for Computational Linguistics*, pages 612–621. 2, 3, 61, 63, 64, 73, 74

Radu Soricut and Sushant Narsale. 2012. Combining quality prediction and system selection for improved automatic translation output. In *Proc. of the 7th Workshop on Statistical Machine Translation*, pages 163–170. 3

Lucia Specia. 2011. Exploiting objective annotations for measuring translation post-editing effort. In *Proc. of 15th Annual Conference of the European Association for Machine Translation*, pages 73–80. 2, 46, 50, 60, 120

Lucia Specia and Atefeh Farzindar. 2010. Estimating machine translation post-editing effort with HTER. In *Proc. of the Workshop Bringing MT to the User: MT Research and the Translation Industry*, pages 33–41. 46

Lucia Specia, Najeh Hajlaoui, Catalina Hallett, and Wilker Aziz. 2011. Predicting machine translation adequacy. In *Proc. of the 13th Machine Translation Summit*, pages 513–520. 49

Lucia Specia, Kim Harris, Frédéric Blain, Aljoscha Burchardt, Viviven Macketanz, Inguna Skadiņa, Matteo Negri, and Marco Turchi. 2017. Translation quality and productivity: A study on rich morphology languages. In *Proc. of the 16th Machine Translation Summit*, pages 55–71. 120

Lucia Specia, Gustavo Paetzold, and Carolina Scarton. 2015. Multi-level translation quality prediction with QuEst++. In *Proc. of the 53rd Annual Meeting of the Association for Computational Linguistics and the 7th International Joint Conference on Natural Language Processing*, pages 115–120. DOI: 10.3115/v1/P15-4020. 118

Lucia Specia, Dhwaj Raj, and Marco Turchi. 2010. Machine translation evaluation vs. quality estimation. *Machine Translation*, 24(1):39–50. DOI: 10.1007/s10590-010-9077-2. 46, 56

Lucia Specia, Kashif Shah, Jose G. C. de Souza, and Trevor Cohn. 2013. QuEst—A translation quality estimation framework. In *Proc. of the 51st Annual Meeting of the Association for Computational Linguistics*, pages 79–84. 95, 118

Lucia Specia, Marco Turchi, Nicola Cancedda, Marc Dymetman, and Nello Cristianini. 2009a. Estimating the sentence-level quality of machine translation systems. In *Proc. of the 13th Annual Conference of the European Association for Machine Translation*, pages 28–37, Barcelona, Spain. 45, 46, 56, 120

Lucia Specia, Marco Turchi, Zhuoran Wang, John Shawe-Taylor, and Craig Saunders. 2009b. Improving the confidence of machine translation quality estimates. In *Proc. of the 12th Machine Translation Summit*. 46

Sanja Štajner, Hannah Béchara, and Horacio Saggion. 2015. A deeper exploration of the standard PB-SMT approach to text simplification and its evaluation. In *Proc. of the 53rd Annual Meeting of the Association for Computational Linguistics and the 7th International Joint Conference on Natural Language Processing*, pages 823–828. DOI: 10.3115/v1/p15-2135 86

Sanja Štajner, Ruslan Mitkov, and Horacio Saggion. 2014. One step closer to automatic evaluation of text simplification systems. In *Proc. of the 3rd Workshop on Predicting and Improving Text Readability for Target Reader Population*, pages 1–10. DOI: 10.3115/v1/w14-1201 84, 85, 86, 89

Sanja Štajner, Maja Popović, and Hannah Béchara. 2016. Quality estimation for text simplification. In *Proc. of the 1st Quality Assessment for Text Simplification Workshop*, pages 15–21. 86, 91, 93, 95

Sanja Štajner, Maja Popović, Horacio Saggion, Lucia Specia, and Mark Fishel. 2016. Shared task on quality assessment for text simplification. In *Proc. of the 1st Quality Assessment for Text Simplification Workshop*, pages 22–31. 87, 120

Josef Steinberger and Karel Ježek. 2009. Evaluation measures for text summarization. *Computing and Informatics*, 28(2):1001–1026. 98

Ruslan Leont'evich Stratonovich. 1960. Conditional Markov processes. *Theory of Probability and its Applications*, 5(2):156–178. DOI: 10.1016/B978-1-4832-3230-0.50041-9. 25

Kaveh Taghipour and Hwee Tou Ng. 2016. A neural approach to automated essay scoring. In *Proc. of the Conference on Empirical Methods on Natural Language Processing*, pages 1882–1891. DOI: 10.18653/v1/D16-1193. 82

Kai Sheng Tai, Richard Socher, and Christopher D. Manning. 2015. Improved semantic representations from tree-structured long short-term memory networks. In *Proc. of the 53rd Annual Meeting of the Association for Computational Linguistics and the 7th International Joint Conference on Natural Language Processing*, pages 1556–1566. DOI: 10.3115/v1/P15-1150. 93

Wilson L. Taylor. 1953. Cloze procedure: A new tool for measuring readability. *Journalism Bulletin*, 30(4):415–433. 90

Arda Tezcan, Veronique Hoste, Bart Desmet, and Lieve Macken. 2015. UGENT-LT3 SCATE system for machine translation quality estimation. In *Proc. of the 10th Workshop on Statistical Machine Translation*, pages 353–360. DOI: 10.18653/v1/W15-3043. 16, 18

Arda Tezcan, Veronique Hoste, and Lieve Macken. 2016. UGENT-LT3 SCATE submission for WMT shared task on quality estimation. In *Proc. of the 1st Conference on Machine Translation*, pages 843–850. DOI: 10.18653/v1/W16-2393. 22, 56

Roy W. Tromble, Shankar Kumar, Franz Och, and Wolfgang Macherey. 2008. Lattice minimum Bayes-risk decoding for statistical machine translation. In *Proc. of the Conference on Empirical Methods on Natural Language Processing*, pages 620–629. DOI: 10.3115/1613715.1613792 8

Marco Turchi, Matteo Negri, and Marcello Federico. 2013. Coping with the subjectivity of human judgements in MT quality estimation. In *Proc. of the 8th Workshop on Statistical Machine Translation*, pages 240–251. 46

Marco Turchi, Matteo Negri, and Marcello Federico. 2014. Data-driven annotation of binary MT quality estimation corpora based on human post-editions. *Machine Translation*, 28(3):281–308. DOI: 10.1007/s10590-014-9162-z. 47, 51, 57

Marco Turchi, Matteo Negri, and Marcello Federico. 2015. MT quality estimation for computer-assisted translation: Does it really help? In *Proc. of the 53rd Annual Meeting of the Association for Computational Linguistics and the 7th International Joint Conference on Natural Language Processing*, pages 530–535. DOI: 10.3115/v1/P15-2087. 47

Marco Turchi, Josef Steinberger, and Lucia Specia. 2012. Relevance ranking for translated texts. In *Proc. of the 16th Annual Conference of the European Association for Machine Translation*, pages 153–160. 48

Nicola Ueffing, José G. C. de Souza, and Gregor Leusch. 2018. Quality estimation for automatically generated titles of eCommerce browse pages. In *Proc. of the Conference of the North American Chapter of the Association for Computational Linguistics: Human Language Technologies*, pages 52–59. 111, 112, 113, 117

Nicola Ueffing and Hermann Ney. 2004. Bayes decision rules and confidence measures for statistical machine translation. In *Proc. of the 4th International Conference on Natural Language Processing*, pages 70–81, Spain. DOI: 10.1007/978-3-540-30228-5_7. 7

Nicola Ueffing and Hermann Ney. 2007. Word-level confidence estimation for machine translation. *Computational Linguistics*, 33(1):9–40. DOI: 10.1162/coli.2007.33.1.9. 7

Ramakrishna Vedantam, C. Lawrence Zitnick, and Devi Parikh. 2015. CIDEr: Consensus-based image description evaluation. In *Proc. of the Conference on Computer Vision and Pattern Recognition*, pages 4566–4575. DOI: 10.1109/cvpr.2015.7299087 110

Ashish Venugopal, Andreas Zollmann, and Stephan Vogel. 2007. An efficient two-pass approach to synchronous-CFG driven statistical MT. In *Proc. of the Conference of the North American Chapter of the Association for Computational Linguistics: Human Language Technologies*, pages 500–507. 8

Tsung-Hsien Wen, Milica Gašić, Nikola Mrkšić, Pei-Hao Su, David Vandyke, and Steve Young. 2015. Semantically conditioned LSTM-based natural language generation for spoken dialogue systems. In *Proc. of the Conference on Empirical Methods on Natural Language Processing*, pages 1711–1721. DOI: 10.18653/v1/d15-1199 109, 110

Frank Wessel, Ralf Schluter, and Hermann Ney. 2000. Using posterior word probabilities for improved speech recognition. In *Proc. of the IEEE International Conference on Acoustics, Speech, and Signal Processing*, pages 1587–1590. DOI: 10.1109/ICASSP.2000.861989. 8

Guillaume Wisniewski, Anil Kumar Singh, Natalia Segal, and François Yvon. 2013. Design and analysis of a large corpus of post-edited translations: Quality estimation, failure analysis and the variability of post-edition. In *Proc. of the 14th Machine Translation Summit*, pages 117–124. 120

Sander Wubben, Antal van den Bosch, and Emiel Krahmer. 2012. Sentence simplification by monolingual machine translation. In *Proc. of the 50th Annual Meeting of the Association for Computational Linguistics*, pages 1015–1024. 82

Deyi Xiong, Min Zhang, and Haizhou Li. 2010. Error detection for statistical machine translation using linguistic features. In *Proc. of the 48th Annual Meeting of the Association for Computational Linguistics*, pages 604–611. 7, 16

Wei Xu, Courtney Napoles, Ellie Pavlick, Quanze Chen, and Chris Callison-Burch. 2016. Optimizing statistical machine translation for text simplification. *Transactions of the Association for Computational Linguistics*, 4:401–415. 82

Torsten Zesch, Michael Wojatzki, and Dirk Scholten-Akoun. 2015. Task-independent features for automated essay grading. In *Proc. of the 10th Workshop on Innovative Use of NLP for Building Educational Applications*, pages 224–232. DOI: 10.3115/v1/w15-0626 82

Hao Zhang and Daniel Gildea. 2008. Efficient multi-pass decoding for synchronous context free grammars. In *Proc. of the 46th Annual Meeting of the Association for Computational Linguistics*, pages 209–217. 8

Ying Zhang, Almut Silja Hildebrand, and Stephan Vogel. 2006. Distributed language modeling for N-best list re-ranking. In *Proc. of the Conference on Empirical Methods on Natural Language Processing*, pages 216–223. DOI: 10.3115/1610075.1610108 8

Daniel Zwillinger and Stephen Kokoska. 1999. *Standard Probability and Statistics Tables and Formulae*. Chapman and Hall/CRC, Boca Raton, FL. 59

Authors' Biographies

LUCIA SPECIA

Lucia Specia is a Professor of Language Engineering in the Department of Computer Science at the University of Sheffield. Her research focuses on various aspects of data-driven approaches to multilingual language processing with a particular interest in multimodal context models for language grounding that has applications in machine translation, quality estimation, and text adaptation. She is the recipient of an ERC Starting Grant on multimodal machine translation (2016–2021) and has been involved in a number of other research projects on machine translation (EC FP7 QTLaunch-Pad and EXPERT, EC H2020 QT21 21, CRACKER) and EC H2020 text adaptation (SIMPATICO). Before joining the University of Sheffield in 2012, she was Senior Lecturer at the University of Wolverhampton (2010–2011) and research engineer at the Xerox Research Centre, France (2008–2009). She received a Ph.D. in Computer Science from the University of São Paulo, Brazil, in 2008.

CAROLINA SCARTON

Carolina Scarton is a Research Associate at the University of Sheffield and a member of the Natural Language Processing Group. She holds a Ph.D. on Quality Estimation of Machine Translation from the University of Sheffield (2017) and her research interests are quality estimation, text simplification, evaluation of NLP task outputs at the document level, and readability assessment. Currently, Dr. Scarton works for the EC H2020 SIMPATICO project, where she develops approaches for sentence simplification. Previously, she was a Marie Skłodowska-Curie Early Stage Researcher working for the EXPERT project on the topic of machine translation at the University of Sheffield (2013–2016).

GUSTAVO HENRIQUE PAETZOLD

Gustavo Henrique Paetzold is an Adjunct Professor at the Federal University of Technology – Paraná. He holds a Ph.D. from the University of Sheffield (2016). His main research interests are text simplification, psycholinguistics, quality estimation, and machine learning applied to natural language processing. Prior to joining the Federal University of Technology, Dr. Paetzold worked as a Research Associate at the University of Sheffield on the EC H2020 SIMPATICO project, where he developed approaches for lexical simplification (2016–2018).

Printed in the United States
by Baker & Taylor Publisher Services